TO ILLUSTRATE THAT

Alistair Brown

A resource for Christian speakers

Christian Focus
Publications Ltd.

Published by
Christian Focus Publications Ltd
Houston, Texas,　　Tain, Ross-shire,
USA　　　　　　Scotland

ISBN   0   906731   85   2
©1989 Alistair Brown

Printed and bound in Great Britain by
Collins, Glasgow

CONTENTS

PREFACE

This book aims to help us to carry biblical truth in our minds. These illustrations are designed to explain various points of doctrine. They follow the example of the Lord Jesus who used every day illustrations as 'windows' for people to understand His message.

Through these 'windows' we hope that you and those you speak to will see something of the Glory of the Person of Christ and experience the power of His truth.

W.H.M.M. 1989.

ACKNOWLEDGMENTS

I would like to express my special thanks to:

— congregations in Livingston and Aberdeen who have received these sermon illustrations, with tolerance and appreciation.

— my wife and children, God's very special gift to me, enabling ministry to others.

— Colin and Kathleen of C. F. P. who have blessed me with their encouragement and theology.

— Leadership Journal of the United States who first inspired me to write down illustrations and who have published an article containing some of the material used in the introduction of this book.

— Jonathan Brentnall for his cartoons, but even more for being a good friend.

A.B.

How To Use This Book . . .

This book is intended as a resource for ministers, teachers, organisation leaders — indeed for anyone who has to give Christian sermons or talks. It is not designed to be read through from beginning to end but to be dipped into as need arises for illustrations on specific topics. Headings are arranged alphabetically to help that process.

Most however, would benefit from reading the introductory chapter on how to use illustrations well. No story is an end in itself, merely a tool to help the speaker make his point. So, no matter how good a story is, the way it is told, combined with a skilful weaving of it into the flow of the message is vital and the ten rules listed in that chapter should help most people.

As you look at the illustrations themselves, you'll see that ninety percent of them are general in character and could be told immediately by anyone. There are a few, however, which appear as my own personal stories. You can still use these in one of two ways. Either tell them as an incident which happened to someone else ('I read recently of a man who...'), or allow them to trigger your memory for something which happened in your own experience and tell of that. (See the introductory chapter for more on 'personalising' stories.)

Perhaps there's no illustration in this collection on the subject you want, or you've already used what does appear. If that's the case, first of all check in case there's another heading which is similar — e.g., there's not a great difference between 'persecution' and 'testing' and you may get help that way. Secondly, with caution, many stories can be used to make quite different points from those I have. For example, under 'Church Growth', there's an illustration about many plugs being joined to the one adaptor, attached to an electric socket. The point made there concerns the danger of overload in church life. By a little rewording, however, to remove the negative aspects of the illustration, it could be used to describe the gifting of the Holy Spirit. Like the different appliances joined to the one socket, various gifts emerge among God's people, but all from the one source (1 Corinthians 12:4-11). If you can allow your imagination to run free, the value of the book can be multiplied many times.

I would suggest you keep a note of the illustrations you use. In truth, this book is partly the product of my own need to do that. Looking through old sermons, I would discover, to my horror, that in the previous Sunday's sermon I had told exactly the same story as I used last year. The congregation either didn't remember, or were too polite to say! Still, it was undesirable and I had to begin to keep a record. As far as these illustrations are concerned, a simple note of 'place and date' of usage at the end of the story should suffice. I should add that I see nothing wrong in repeating a good illustration after a significant time lag. If it's so good that the congregation do remember, then they'll be glad to hear it again!

This collection of illustrations is copyright in the usual way, but there is no restriction on the telling of individual stories in talks and sermons.

Illustrate Well! . . .

Illustrations are wonderful tools for making a sermon 'live' to a congregation. But, as with all tools, they can be used either well or badly. Poorly used illustrations don't enhance the message and may even confuse the hearer. Here are some rules to help guide speakers in the right direction with their illustrations.

1. A story must really illustrate what you're trying to explain.

A tailor might wish he could adapt his client's body to fit a ready-made suit but that thought is, of course, ludicrous. Yet preachers face a temptation to try for something similar by adapting the sermon to fit the great story they want to tell.

A story I hear often in sermons these days concerns the captain of a battlecruiser who keeps exchanging terse messages with a vessel dead ahead, each telling the other to move aside. The denouement of the story is that the other 'vessel' turns out to be a lighthouse. That illustration seems to me to belong best in highlighting our need to give way to the lordship of Christ, but I have heard it used as a minister was being introduced to a new congregation (who was to give way there I wonder?), and — I confess — I have used it in a speech at a wedding reception stating that it was a wise man who knew when to give way to his wife!

Which has priority? Is it the illustration or the message to be preached? If the former is allowed too much latitude, we may lose the point which ought to be made.

2. The link with the main message must be clear.

I will never forget the horror of finding myself half way through a dramatic illustration and realising I had no idea whatsoever how that story applied to the sermon I was preaching. Something must have been in my mind when I'd jotted it down in my notes, but I hadn't written down any link back to the main text. I had to cover the situation as best I could, but I'm perfectly sure that if I, the preacher, couldn't see a link, the congregation didn't either! These days I always make crystal clear in my notes how the illustration fits. So if one phrase is vital to make the transition back to the message, I write it down and underline it both in the illustration and in the linking sentence.

3. An illustration mustn't be unnecessarily long.

Some people have a gift of story-telling and the humour they can inject in spinning a yarn can greatly enliven the message. Sometimes though an illustration can be tediously long. Again, what we need to sort out is priority and that must not go to the story no matter how good it is.

One tale I heard a preacher tell must have lasted some fifteen minutes. Considering the whole sermon was only about twenty five minutes, that was quite a chunk of the whole. Probably everyone remembered the story, but not too many the rest of the sermon.

Jesus did tell several lengthy parables (talents, prodigal son, labourers in the vineyard, etc), but there are also many which are very short. John 14:18 contains a masterly illustration in very few words: 'I will not leave you as orphans; I will come to you.' The connotations of being abandoned and alone are all there, with the reassurance that that would not be the disciples' experience, and all in one sentence. Luke 5:36-39 has three parables in just four verses.

There is only so much time in a sermon — give no more to any one illustration than it needs or deserves.

4. Never risk embarrassment for others.

The preacher is allowed to tell stories against himself, but to embarrass someone else can destroy relationships.

The classic failure for preachers is with their own children. One minister's daughter said that as a child she and her sisters dreaded each Sunday wondering what personal family stories about them would be told to the whole congregation.

The preacher who uses pastoral experiences to provide living stories to illustrate the message will soon find not too many want to seek his help. Even telling of people from a previous pastoral charge will warn many off who don't want anyone ever to know their secrets.

If personal stories like this are to be used, then express permission must be obtained first. And that must not be had under a quasi-spiritual blackmail of 'I know you'll want to help others who are struggling as you were ...'.

5. Don't bore and annoy people with trivia.

I've told of how I still keep a little stool which is too wobbly to allow anyone to sit on it. The point is that I keep it because many years ago at school I made it in a wood-work class. Since I made it, it matters to me, and from there it's easy to speak about God's love for this broken world.

That's acceptable, even although the topic of the illustration is not of great importance, but what's not acceptable is to litter an illustration with trivial details.

Suppose I'd related the illustration of the stool like this: 'Keeping a tidy home is an ideal for which we should all strive diligently. That means there's always dusting and cleaning to be done, along with sorting through the things we collect over the years. Do you know, as I sat in my study the other day, reading the mail, studying the Bible, and praying for each one of you, my eye strayed from time to time over to the corner of the room? There, almost in darkness, sat something which is very old now, and could so easily have been cleared out years ago...' If that was how it was told, by now the congregation would all have fallen asleep with boredom, and they still wouldn't have heard that it's a stool which sits in the corner. Does the lecture on tidiness and the details of the pastor's work routine help the illustration? Not one bit — therefore, they shouldn't be there.

An overweight man makes slow progress. So does an overweight illustration. Keep the story crisp.

6. The story should never be too striking.

That sounds strange advice, for normally an illustration should be as striking as possible, but it's possible to go 'over the top'.

I was preaching one time on the importance of a daily, vital relationship with God but wanted to stress an essential pre-requisite. So, dropping my voice and lowering my head, I continued like this: 'My friends, I have to tell you in all seriousness that there was a time when I did not love my wife at all.' The congregation began to go very quiet. 'It wasn't that love "burned low". If I was honest I would have to say I felt nothing at all for Alison.' The hush by now was awesome. People told me later they thought some terrible confession was coming next! 'Yes,' I went on, 'and it continued like that for twenty one years... Then — at that age — I met her!' There was one more moment of silence and then thankful guffaws of laughter as people realised I'd led them on.

I continued by speaking about how we cannot love someone we haven't even met — and so before we can have a living, loving relationship with God we have to meet him, i.e., be born again. (A revised — toned down! — version of this illustration appears in the section on 'Worship'.)

However, after such a heart-stopping illustration, by now no-one was listening to me! People were still chortling away and that continued through most of the rest of the sermon. After it was all over, the illustration was a great talking point but who remembered the application?

7. Be funny, but don't crack jokes.

Most preachers can't tell jokes and they shouldn't anyway. The pulpit is not a comedian's platform.

Yet a careful use of humour can instantly bring back the congregation's wandering attention, and help a message 'live'. Some can tell humorous stories. The golden rule here is to make sure the story does move the sermon in the right direction and isn't just being told because it's funny.

I have used one about a department store which employed an efficiency expert. He kept changing things around, and every day departments were moved to new parts of the building as the expert tried out his ideas. After some two weeks of this an elderly lady approached the doorman and in a rather exasperated tone of voice complained she could no longer find the millinery department and could he please tell her where it was. He replied: 'No, madam, I cannot, however, if you will just stand there for a moment, I'm sure you'll see it go past!'

That was a story used in a sermon on 'Change' and helped the introduction which was about the pace of modern life and the bewildering effect it can have on us.

More often, I prefer simply to inject a humorous comment into a story, otherwise serious. I've used marriage many times as an example of a change of status (to illustrate the change when we make a vow to Christ). One time I found myself saying, 'Before the wedding, Alison was my friend. After the wedding she was my wife and not my friend any more...' Said in the right tone of voice, the congregation laughed, and still saw the real point being made.

Humour which does not distract is a great tool.

8. Don't annoy people.

Following on from the last point, one certain way to annoy most of your listeners is to tell 'in' jokes, i.e., to make remarks which are relevant and funny only to a section of those listening. Vague references to events or people quite unknown to all but a few are very irritating for the rest.

If you must tell a story involving the circumstances of an individual known only to some present, patiently explain all the necessary details so that everyone can share equally in the humour and have the same opportunity to grasp the point which follows from it.

Another source of annoyance I discovered by the complaints made to me later! I had seen a fairly recently released film at the cinema. That film contained a very moving sequence which was perfect for illustrating how guilt can burden someone's life and then how he can be wonderfully freed when that guilt is taken from him. I described that scene with drama and enthusiasm, giving as much graphic detail as possible and allowing the story to build to a marvellous climax. Then, of course, I applied it to the message I was preaching. But afterwards quite a few said they'd planned to go and see that film and now I'd ruined it for them. They'd never be able to enjoy it properly since I had told them what was going to happen! Mistakenly they had thought I had given away the main plot, which I hadn't. Nevertheless, the point remains: an illustration which annoys or distracts does not help your hearers to appreciate the message you're preaching.

9. Make your stories personal, if possible.

It is deceitful and therefore sinful to pretend

that what happened to someone else actually happened to you. That can never be right and God cannot honour such a practice.

Nevertheless, rather than tell of something you read about another, it is often much better to be able to tell a similar story which really did happen to you. Instead of describing a near-death accident which happened to some other person, has nothing like that ever been your experience? Or, if the person you read about hesitated before proposing marriage, did you? Have you heard of someone getting lost — well, haven't you ever been lost? Allow someone else's story to trigger your own memory.

Almost always you will be able to tell your own story with far greater vigour and 'life' than you could ever muster for an account of what happened to another person.

10. Put effort into telling the illustration.

If a story is worth telling, it's worth telling well. Don't use a boring monotone. Allow your voice to dramatise the story. If the illustration includes dialogue, try using different 'voices' for the different people speaking. Allow pauses for a point to sink in, or for the congregation to appreciate the tension of the situation you are describing. If the story is funny, allow the people to laugh — don't squash that by pressing on too quickly. Let your facial expressions play a part and, of course, gestures as well.

You're not meant to be an actor, but communicating the greatest of truths should grip you with a passion and vibrancy which comes through naturally in the way you speak, and that will be specially so as you tell an illustration.

Used well, illustrations make the difference between incomprehension and understanding and between boredom and vitality, and thus between the forgettable and the memorable message. But keep to basic rules like these, or what you attain may be the opposite of what you desire.

Atonement . . .

One of Scotland's cities, Aberdeen, is bounded by a fast-flowing river. Around one hundred years ago, pupils in one area of the city needed to cross the river to reach their school. To get them there, one of the first ever iron suspension bridges was constructed, and is still known as the Shakkin' Briggie (Shaking Bridge).

More recently that bridge has been allowed to fall into disrepair but moves are afoot to have it restored. There is, however, one fundamental problem with that which will be hard to overcome. Over the years the flow of the river has eroded the bank, widening the river bed. So the bridge which originally crossed from one side to the other now finishes some fifty feet short of the far bank. You can't cross a bridge which doesn't touch both banks.

It's because Jesus is both God and man that only He can save us. He alone could speak and act for God, with a nature untainted by sin. He alone could represent man, dying our death on the cross. Both natures were needed — without one, atonement could not have happened. He was the God-man and so is our only Mediator and Saviour. He is the bridge touching both banks and only by Him can we cross over.

Awe . . .

The more we get to know God's great power, the less cocky and casual we will be.

Trawlermen can make a very good living from the sea. There are some who are millionaires while still in their twenties. They can walk into a car showroom, hand over cash and drive out in an expensive model. You'd think they would love the sea, for it brings many of them such a very high standard of living.

But many (perhaps most) are frightened. Some have lost a father or a brother at sea, or have perhaps been washed overboard themselves but somehow survived. They know how near death they can come. Some will speak of how they feel sick every time they are within twenty four hours of setting sail.

These men gain a lot from the sea but they also know the sea's power and they have more than just respect for it. There is real fear.

Our loving Father doesn't want us to live frightened of Him. Yet, as we sense more and more of His might and realise more and more of what He can do, there will be a sense of our unworthiness, and a great awe upon us about our God.

Baptism . . .

Normally, people are allowed to consider whether or not baptism is right for them and consequently when it would be right for them.

You could liken it to a school with a liberal attitude about school uniform. A uniform would exist, but it would be left to each pupil to decide whether or not to wear it. It would be nice if he did but there is no compulsion of any kind.

Now, with baptism, that's fine if baptism really is optional in that way. We can allow people to decide for themselves.

But nowhere in the New Testament is baptism portrayed as being optional. Very clearly it is commanded of everyone who is converted.

For a man, marriage usually means security, shopping done for him, regular meals, good company, clothes which are washed and ironed, and a warm bed at night.

All of those are true — but not one of them comes even near to the central importance of marriage.

Some things taught about baptism are like that — true, but not central to its meaning.

Yes, we do it because that is to follow the example of Jesus. Yes, baptism means the convert thus witnesses to his new faith. Yes, baptism is like a soldier putting on his uniform, enlisting in the army. These are all true, but none taught in Scripture as the reason for baptism. The washing away of sin and union with Christ are far more biblical ideas. (Acts 22:16; Galatians 3:27).

In Romans 6 Paul says the baptised believer is buried with Christ and raised with Christ. That is true because he is now at one with Jesus. What is true of Jesus is true of him.

When a couple marry, quite apart from all the romantic and spiritual associations, they enter into a legal oneness.

The husband's assets and liabilities become also now the wife's assets and liabilities. What he owns and what he owes become also what she owns and what she owes. What is true of him becomes true of her.

So, in the oneness with Christ in baptism, what is true of Jesus is true now of the believer. Jesus died to sin and so the believer has also died to sin. Jesus was raised to new life and so therefore has the believer been raised. Thus in union with Christ — and only thus — does the believer die and rise in baptism.

When the USA choose a new President, he's elected, he accepts, but later there's still the swearing-in ceremony.

The troops parade in their finest uniforms. Top officials and their wives appear in even greater finery. Some of the public and press are there but millions more round the world watch on TV. All of these are witnesses to this occasion.

Then the new President is called on to uphold

the Constitution, to defend the nation, to seek its good and so on. In response he makes solemn and public promises about these matters.

That is partly what baptism is. The call to membership of the kingdom of God has been given. In response to that call of Christ, baptism is a solemn confession and acceptance of Jesus as Saviour and Lord.

Change . . .

There is a very strange paradox — when night-time comes you don't want to go to bed, yet when morning comes you don't want to get out of bed!

The explanation of that paradox is that none of us likes change. It's too much effort to get organised for bed, so we prefer to sit up late. It's far too cosy and comfortable in bed ever to want to leave it and face the day. So we prefer things as they are rather than change.

Church life is no different. In our styles of worship, and in the cosiness of our small congregations, we get to like things just as they are and, despite our words, deep down we don't really want to change.

We can face a similar difficulty in evangelism. People may well give intellectual assent to the gospel but the truth is that they don't want to change. They've become used to the old life and even though it doesn't satisfy, the security given by sameness seems better than the effort change would require.

A person with very broad feet can find buying new shoes is a nightmare as they never fit. Yet, inevitably, he must buy some shoes, so takes the best he can find. Then the next few weeks are agony as these shoes pinch and squeeze the feet. Eventually, though, the shoes adjust and can become comfortable.

If, somehow, it was possible to make shoes last forever, he'd prefer that. The pain of breaking in a new pair would make the broad-footed person opt every time for sticking with the familiar old ones.

Likewise, in our lives and in our churches, we usually opt for the old, familiar (though perhaps wrong) ways, rather than have to 'break ourselves in' to new habits and patterns.

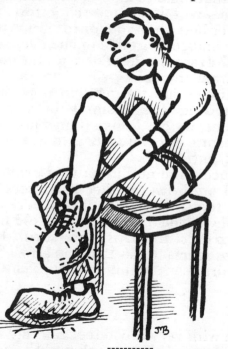

During World War I troops were literally bogged down for months in trenches, never moving significantly forward or backward. However, the war was won only when they got out of the trenches and pressed home the attack, horrendous though the casualties were.

Though it will cost us our cosiness and our comfort we have to resist the temptation to dig in with 'how things are' in the church and press on to win new victories for the Lord.

One of the great joys of returning from holiday is the first night back in your own bed. On holiday you may well have slept in far more expensive or far newer beds, but there's nothing quite like crawling into your own personal, creaky bed. It fits your shape. The springs dig in to familiar places. The hollow is one you have moulded yourself.

In life generally all of us like the known, the familiar, the things we have shaped. We can acknowledge that something else might be better but we feel safe with what we already have. We like it that way.

Jesus calls His people to abandon the old and the safe and to risk venturing out with Him. It won't be comfortable, nor at first will it feel secure, but at last great things will be achieved as we do the work He gives us.

One weekend, Winston Churchill and his Parliamentary colleague Mrs Bessie Braddock (renowned for her large frame and hard looks) were guests at a country house.

In the evening, Churchill had more than a reasonable share of alcohol and became somewhat inebriated. As he made his way rather unsteadily to his bedroom, he encountered Mrs Braddock in the corridor. She was rather shocked at his condition: 'Mr Churchill, you're drunk,' she said.

'Mrs Braddock,' he replied, 'you're ugly! But I'll be sober in the morning!'

Our faults may be many, but as long as there's a chance of change, let's not lose hope!

If you are paying a visit to someone and you're invited to 'Sit down' you probably ask: 'Where would you like me to sit...?'

The reason for asking isn't that you doubt the strength of some of the furniture to carry your weight, but the recognition that people become accustomed to having certain chairs as their own and that they don't really like to be put out of their own seat. Of course, out of politeness, nothing would ever be said but people would prefer to keep things the way they're used to.

In church life too we allow things to settle into familiar patterns. We dislike change whether or not it is reasonable.

If all the chairs in someone's home are identical, logically it doesn't seem important who sits where, but yet it is to those who live there. They have their routine and don't want shifted from it.

Likewise, resistance to change in church life is at a deeper level than that of logic!

Christlikeness . . .

Being a Christian should be impossible to conceal.

Sometimes visitors to a lighthouse are allowed to climb to the top. Round and round, up and up they go, until they reach the small room at the top which contains the light. There the lighthouse keeper will be able to tell countless stories of how that light saved lives during storms.

Sure enough, return at night-time and the beam will be shining out into the darkness, visible for miles even in poor weather. It would be virtually impossible for anyone to miss that light. It is so bright.

Well, in truth there is precisely one way in which that light will not be seen — and that is if it isn't lit. That's the only way.

That's how it is for us too. If we are not shining out in the darkness for Christ and if it is not clear that we are His, then it is simply because we aren't 'lit' — the light of Christ isn't in us.

Is Jesus really Lord over your life? Is He your purpose for living, the goal of your life?

One of the surprises you get if you visit a lighthouse is to discover how small the light actually is. There's nothing tremendously powerful about the size of the bulbs.

The secret of the great power of the light lies in the reflectors and lenses — highly polished metal and glass that bounce the light round and round and then out into the night sky, thus shining for miles.

Let that metal become tarnished. Let that glass become stained. Then the light beam can hardly pass through and only the palest of lights will emerge.

Perhaps in many of our lives that's the problem. Yes, Christ is there. He's been there for years, but we've allowed our lives to become tarnished and stained with our sinfulness, lethargy, and carelessness and now only the dimmest of lights reaches out. Our lives have become so very much like those of everyone else and only the palest of images of Christ now shines through.

Failure to show the light of Christ in our lives is dangerous for our world.

If a lighthouse fails, then ships may founder and lives be lost. No longer do sailors have any sure idea of where the dangerous rocks are situated.

Likewise when Christians cease to be lights to this world, then no-one can be sure any more just what is right and what is wrong. If Christ's light doesn't shine through us, then this world will drift into greater and greater danger, nearer and nearer the 'rocks' and people won't even know it.

Church Growth . . .

If I go to the doctor with a severe headache, I don't expect to be given a prescription for a cough bottle. Or if I go, having caught some virus, I don't expect to be told to buy some bandages. I expect that the treatment I receive will do

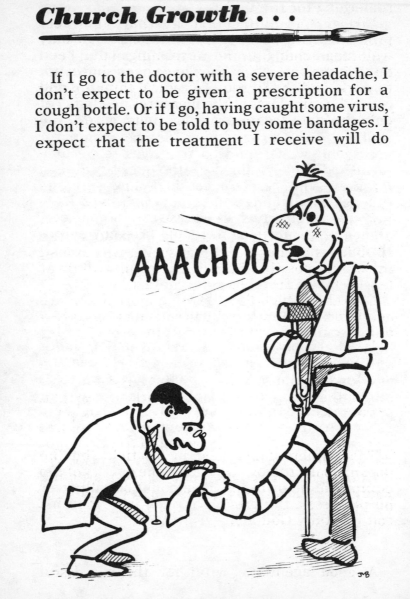

AAACHOO!

something for the illness I have.

Likewise in the church we have to meet problems with appropriate solutions. That may well mean changing the ways things have been done in the past where they have been shown not to work, and that'll require radical thinking and courage to implement the measures needed. Yet only the right treatment will bring a cure.

It is possible to take one electric socket and by the joining together of several adaptors make many different plugs all work from that socket. Yet that is also very dangerous, for there is a great likelihood that the demand made by the appliances connected to that socket will exceed the output possible from it. The result will be at least a blown fuse but could in fact be a fire.

Churches which keep loading more and more activity on to the same church members or on to a never-changing church structure risk similar disaster. The members may blow a spiritual fuse and be unable to do any further work, and the overloaded and inflexible church system will begin to damage the church's work rather than prosper it.

The farmer plants seed in his field, but he doesn't make it grow. No matter the quality of the equipment he owns, or the amount of willpower he possesses, the growth as such is beyond his control. Only God gives growth.

A good agenda is vital for the successful

functioning of any committee or business meeting. If that hasn't been formulated clearly, or is not known to these attending the meeting, then time can be wasted on trivialities. People must know the goals they are to meet if good work is to be done.

Likewise, if church members are unclear about their mission, then they will become distracted into countless activities, which may be good enough in themselves but are irrelevant to the central task of the church.

Imagine you are in a foreign country, one where you don't know either the language or the geography. So, by yourself, you could never find your way around.

Happily, however, you have a guide. So, everything should be all right. You ought to have a very pleasant time in that land.

Two things though could go wrong.

One is if the guide were to decide to take you to the wrong places, to locations to which you weren't meant to go.

The second is if the guide himself were to get lost. If that happened, then the tour party could end up anywhere by taking wrong turnings.

If you can't believe the guide will take you to worthwhile places, or you don't think he knows the way, then you're not going to enjoy the trip.

Church members are not foreigners who know nothing about the land and ministers are not guides who are supposed to know everything.

But the analogy of people being on a journey where there's a break-down of confidence or a fear about what lies ahead is still relevant. For that can happen to congregations, especially at a time of growth and change. So, leaders must be people who are loved and respected if they are to inspire trust, and they must communicate well. The people need to be told by their leaders what some of the 'destinations' are which lie ahead, in order to give them confidence.

Commission . . .

A reporter has a life many would envy, for he has the opportunity to meet many fascinating people: top sports stars, famous people of pop with a string of No.1 hits, the rich and powerful, heads of state, etc. The journalist can get alongside these people and come to know them.

What gives him the right to meet these stars others see only at a distance? Is it because the journalist is a particularly clever or fine person? Is it because he's as gifted and popular as the star?

Certainly not! The reporter is no-one special, but he has the right to meet these top names only because of who sends him. His newspaper gives him a pass and sets him the task of holding an interview. Because of who he represents he does work which otherwise would not be possible for him.

Our strength to serve God in this world lies in who has sent us. With God's commission and God's authority, we can have courage and boldness to do great things.

God never sends us out alone to do His work. He promises to be with us (Judges 6:16; Matthew 28:20).

There are however, two senses in which someone can be with another person.

1 — As a spectator

If you are playing in a golf match, and in the

crowd there stands Jack Nicklaus watching, that may be nice but won't improve your score because he can't hit the shots for you.

A by-stander is with you but makes no difference to how well you perform.

2 — As a participant

Perhaps as a child you were given a task which seemed more than you could manage — digging the garden, mowing the lawn, clearing out the attic, tidying your bedroom! The work was hard, difficult, tiring and perhaps boring. As time went on, you became increasingly lethargic and your energy was disappearing.

Then father or mother took pity on you and said: 'Come on, let's do this together!' Suddenly, the job was much easier, almost fun. Someone else was helping and what seemed to be taking hours was over in minutes. Someone was with you to work.

God is never with us as a spectator, always as a participant. With Him, great things can be done.

Commitment . . .

There's many a man who knows he ought to propose marriage, but puts it off. It isn't that he lacks love for the young woman he has befriended, nor is he frightened of a negative answer to his proposal. Rather, the problem is a fear of commitment to one individual. He realises how serious a thing that is, and shies away from it, perhaps for another year, perhaps forever... Fear can halt commitment.

That may be what stops you coming to Jesus. It's not lack of knowledge or belief in the gospel message, but fear of giving all else up for Christ. However, no-one yet had a happy marriage without rising above that inner fear and a similar abandonment to Jesus is essential in order to find the 'real life' He promises.

A couple don't fall in love on their wedding day. They're already in love. The wedding, then, is the act of commitment to each other because of that love. It is their response to what they now see to be true about their relationship.

Jesus pledged His life to us when he hung on our cross, taking our sin, and now He calls all who want to accept this to acknowledge it in a serious and deliberate way. See Romans 10:9-10. This public testimony to Jesus is the right response.

18

Consistency . . .

The 1987 Portugese Grand Prix will be remembered as the race in which Frenchman Alain Prost set a new record of twenty eight wins in Formula One racing.

What, in time, will not be recalled is that the race should have marked a revival for Ferrari racing in the person of Gerhard Berger. He led Prost for the whole race, though the latter was gaining lap by lap towards the end. Yet, the TV commentators were able to say confidently that Berger was far enough ahead that he would win, causing tremendous celebrations in Italy because of Ferrari's prominence. Even when the gap between leader and second place Prost was down to two seconds, still Berger should not have been caught as there were only two laps to go.

Suddenly, Berger spun his car and Prost was through and setting that record win. The pressure had got to the Austrian and he'd become careless and taken a corner badly. One commentator remarked: 'Now all he'll be awarded is the Freedom of Italian Prisons!'

A race isn't over until the end is reached. In our Christian lives, it's possible to become careless even when in sight of the end and to spoil what went before. Gideon, Samson, Elijah, are just a few great figures of the Bible who have done that. Paul was determined it should not happen to him (1 Corinthians 9:27).

Seve Ballesteros could give a talk on 'Playing Par Golf' — he can play like that and even better.

But would anyone listen to *you* talk on that subject...? Can *you* keep scoring that well?

When our lives match our words, then people will begin to listen to us as we tell of the change Christ makes.

Contentment . . .

When you are given a box of chocolates, you may well think: 'I'll eat just one today and keep the rest for later.' But then, that one tasted so good... 'Just one more,' you promise yourself.

By the end of the evening they've all gone, haven't they!? By that time you're wishing you had another box... You see, eating one satisfied a desire, but it also created a desire for more.

The man who thinks he'll be content if only his bank account could show one thousand pounds is satisfied for only a very short time when he achieves it. For the very achieving of it simply triggers an even bigger desire. Now he wants two thousand pounds, and after that it'll be five thousand pounds, then ten thousand pounds, and so on. It's the same with other things in life too. The desires simply grow. The more we have the more we want.

Contentment is never to be found in satisfying all our wants.

A young child may well be given a 'shapes ball' with which to play — one of these toys with many differently cut holes and objects to match each. The idea is for the child to learn to push the right object through each hole and, of course, each will go only through one hole. The triangle won't pass through a circular hole, nor a star shape through an oval hole and so on.

Initially toddlers have so much frustration. They can't get it right and they try to force a shape through the wrong hole. Naturally they get nowhere doing that.

Eventually they do learn and then the game becomes fun — the whole game begins to 'work' for the child.

Our lives were shaped by God for God and it is impossible to find satisfaction and contentment

unless we're in union with him. Without God, we're like the child who constantly tries to force the shape through the wrong hole and knows only frustration. Peace can come only by 'fitting' our lives to the manufacturer's design.

Perhaps at some church outing you will have entered an adults' race. If so, then you may have found that those holding the finishing line have mischievously started running away from you just as you were about to reach the end of the race. You thought you were within reach of your goal but suddenly it started receding from you.

That's exactly how it seems for so many today. The harder they chase happiness and contentment in ambition, wealth, possessions, and human relationships, the faster they seem to go away from them.

A decorator may be engaged to paint a home in striking and bold colours and does exactly as he is told. The result may not appeal to passers-by who could shout their criticisms, but what does that matter to the decorator? Will their comments get him down? No, for those who took him on and chose the colours are pleased with his work and the decorator can therefore be satisfied with what he has done.

The person who finds contentment in life will be the one who pleases the God who made him and called him. What do others' opinions matter?

Counsel . . .

The elderly lady had to go into hospital with circulation difficulties in one leg. Even before she was admitted she knew there was a possibility that the leg would have to be amputated.

Visitors called around that time and many seemed to know of someone else who'd had a similar problem. With a cheery smile, one would say: 'Oh yes, my next door neighbour had to go in with that.' 'And what happened to her?' the lady would enquire, looking for encouragement. 'Yes, and they had to cut off both legs,' would be the reply. Or, another would say: 'I had a grandfather

with that problem...' 'And..?' asked the patient. 'And he died with it...,' the so-called friend would continue.

These visitors were making every attempt to identify with the elderly lady's trouble but they had no positive testimony to bring. To do good you must have both.

The Apostle Paul, for example, knew that. Therefore, he could write to the Corinthians, sharing his own great trials but also testifying to God's deliverance and know that his message would bring them comfort (2 Corinthians 1:3-11).

Criticism . . .

Many will have had the experience of working or living beside someone and, at first, thinking her to be on top of life. She seems to have everything under control, to have no problems whatsoever, to be the master of every situation.

Then, perhaps after many years, something happens which gives you some more insight into that person's situation and you discover that behind the scenes there was always some strain or difficulty for her. Perhaps she gave hours every day to nurse an ageing and infirm relative; perhaps she cared for a handicapped child; perhaps she was still deeply hurt from the loss of a close family member years before.

Suddenly, with this knowledge you see that individual, as it were, through new eyes. Now there's an understanding of the strains and tensions she has been under, all previously unknown to you.

That kind of situation should be remembered when we feel words of criticism or condemnation coming to our lips. Sometimes a person behaves in a particular way because he or she faces tensions of which we are ignorant. Nothing may be obvious on the surface but one day we may learn of the struggle borne without being told to others.

There is a common but illegal practice at rugby lineouts. As the ball is thrown in, one player levers himself up on the shoulder of his opponent. That has the double advantage of restraining his opposite number by holding him down and, in so doing, lifting himself up higher, hopefully to catch the ball.

Many condemn and 'pull others down' with their words or actions, feeling somehow that in so doing they can advance themselves, raise themselves a little higher.

Discipleship . . .

If you starve a plant of adequate light or water, you may not completely kill it but you will certainly stunt it and hinder its growth. If you then bring it out into the light and give it the right amount of water, then suddenly it's going to shoot upwards. Now it has the elements it needs. Now it can become the plant it was meant to be.

The Christian starved (for whatever reason) of things like time with God, Bible study, Christian fellowship, opportunities for Christian service, will be a stunted, immature Christian. Rectify these matters, however, and he will quickly advance a long way in the faith.

When it's the middle of winter, with cold temperatures and possibly snow on the ground, a garden requires virtually no attention or work. It's 'dead', or nearly so. When spring comes, though, suddenly 'life' is there — what a joy that is! Yet, both bulbs and weeds begin to emerge through the soil. Somehow you don't get one without the other, and it will demand considerable work and effort to keep things in order.

So it is when someone becomes a Christian. Before then that person was 'dead' spiritually and — in a sense — no problem. Let spiritual 'life' begin, and joy though that is, more mature Christians must not be surprised to discover that the convert has many difficulties which exist alongside his new faith. That's not the time to 'write him off' but to get close and help him sort these things out. It's hard work but the result is worth it.

If you love someone you want to please that person. You want to bring happiness into his or her life. That will mean you make an effort to discover what the individual likes or dislikes and act accordingly.

So a new wife will quickly learn what meal her husband particularly appreciates and include that in her choice frequently and exclude the things which don't evoke a positive response! Likewise a husband will perhaps look for hints concerning which perfume his wife likes, and avoid in future those left untouched on a dressing table.

To please necessitates discovering what delights the other and then practising that.

If we love Jesus and want to please Him, the principle is the same: discover His will and practice it.

Most people begin the Christian life with great enthusiasm — praying for long periods, Bible reading diligently, absorbing Christian literature and so on. However, as time goes by they can become complacent and forget these disciplines. It's as if they don't sense any long term importance for them.

That's like children learning to swim. When

they first begin they need armbands or a rubber ring but later they feel they can manage fine by their own efforts and dispense with these aids.

Christianity isn't like swimming — it's more like free-fall parachuting. What kind of landings would you have if you decided you didn't need a parachute any more!?

Real discipleship does not involve becoming independent of God but more acutely aware of your need of His help at every moment.

Most dogs love to have a stick thrown to find and bring back to be thrown again. Sometimes the dog will set off just as the owner is in the act of throwing, heading feverishly in the direction he thinks it will go, never pausing to look. That stick may, in fact, land somewhere quite different and on those occasions it's completely lost to the dog. He'll never find it looking in the wrong place.

How often are we so busy doing what we think to be 'God's work' that we never noticed He didn't want us to go in that direction? We just set off in the way we assumed to be right. So we're hunting furiously and fruitlessly for a blessing God cannot give that activity, for He wanted us elsewhere.

A plant which has roots going only an inch or two below the surface is easily destroyed. If the wind blows hard it may fall flat, or if the sun shines it may be burned up.

To survive, those roots need to go down deep. Only then is the plant properly 'anchored' in the soil and only then can it reach down for moisture when the top layers are dry.

That's why Paul speaks of the Christian being 'rooted and built up' in Jesus (Colossians 2:7). A surface relationship with Jesus will prove useless when times get tough.

For a child, every birthday is a milestone. It means something new. Now he's able to do something else. Children are so desperate to grow up!

A like desire to 'grow up' in Christ should be in every Christian — a desire to learn new things, reach new milestones, be able to do more for Him.

An unfloored attic requires great caution from anyone moving around in it. Care is needed to stand only on the joists, the wooden beams which run across it. The rest looks safe but in fact is little more than the thin plasterboard which forms the ceilings of the rooms below. If any weight at all is put on that, the person may come crashing through. The danger is that it looks secure, but it isn't.

So it is with many people's Christianity. First appearances would suggest everything is fine — the right language, habits, dress, and statement of experience are all there. But that seemingly secure commitment may be very thin when put under any strain or stress, easily broken by the hardships of normal life.

Some books have the shiniest and most attractive of covers. The wording on that cover may impress you greatly but buy the book, begin to read and you find the contents lack the brilliance of the cover. The inside doesn't match the glossy exterior.

Some plead a strong commitment to Jesus, but, get to know them better, and you find that their lives don't live up to that closer scrutiny. The first impressions are quickly dissolved.

It was the Boys' Open Golf Championship at St. Andrews, staged over the Eden course. Most of the young competitors on the opening tee were nervous, anxious, never having played in any tournament so significant.

One fifteen year old had a different attitude. He was a well-built lad, strong and tough, and clearly he knew in advance that this was going to be his day. He'd dressed in the neatest of clothes: bright slacks, real golf sweater and brand-new golf shoes. While most struggled with rather dilapidated golf bags over their shoulders, this fellow had a shiny leather golf bag — not that he was carrying it, for he had hired a caddy for the occasion.

On the tee, out came the clubs themselves. There were no rusty old irons for him but a very new, shiny, matched set.

This lad had style. Everything about him spoke the message that he was master of the course, the one who would win that event.

With all the panache he could muster, the lad lined up his opening tee shot. There was a little hitch of the trousers, a waggle of the club. Back he pulled the driver, round his shoulders and down it came with enormous force. Bang! The ball soared off the tee...took a sharp right turn and landed right in the middle of the railway sheds alongside the course (still there in those days). That was out of bounds. One or two unruly lads sniggered quietly in the background.

At the word of command, however, the caddy fetched out another brand new ball and the large lad lined up his second tee shot on that opening hole. Bang! Again the ball soared off the tee...and again it took a sharp right turn, and landed in the railway sheds. Another ball out of bounds and this time there was no sniggering but delighted chuckles from those watching.

Finally he hit his third tee shot. This time it did

not soar off the tee. The fellow topped it and it trundled some one hundred yards along the ground. But at least he was now on his way — a rather dejected and humbled figure.

He'd arrived with such confidence. It was all going to be so easy. The reality was something else.

Many enter into Christianity with all the confidence in the world that this is going to be the cure-all for their problems and that they're going to find life suddenly so much simpler and more pleasant.

That's how they set out but it doesn't take very long until they find that instead life may become more demanding and difficult than before. No problems disappear automatically and following Jesus turns out to require pain and sacrifice daily (Luke 9:23). The reality of life with Jesus can be very different from our expectations.

For a man, getting married can be a devastating experience. Now he can't just:
— toss his dirty clothes down anywhere;
— leave a tide mark around the bath;
— squeeze the toothpaste tube from the top;
— change his socks once a week.

Because someone else's wishes have to be considered there must be changes.

That's how it is entering into life with another person. How much more radical the changes when you share your life with the Kings of Kings and Lord of Lords?

If a child is adopted into a family, then that newcomer comes under certain obligations that go with belonging to that family, with having those particular parents.

There are obligations too on the person who joins God's family. Life can't simply continue as before.

The birds which migrate in the autumn, heading up into the air and turning south, cannot 'know' in which land or in which tree they're going to find a new home.

Yet they go anyway. The security of this country is left behind and they follow the inner urging to seek somewhere else, even though it's unseen to them.

So it is when anyone commits his life to Jesus. It is a commitment to the unseen, trusting Christ to organise the future (2 Corinthians 5:7).

Discipline . . .

If a child carved his initials in the paintwork of his father's car, then very likely he wouldn't be sitting comfortably for a while.

He wouldn't have been smacked to get something out of the dad's system, to satisfy some need for vengeance. The reason for his punishment is to ensure he gets the message loud and clear that that kind of behaviour is totally unacceptable and that he must never do it again. The father loves his child and therefore disciplines him in order that he will learn to live the right way.

As Hebrews 12:5-11 makes clear, only if God didn't love us would he let us drift on any old way. The very existence of His discipline is proof of His love.

If you require a piece of metal for an unimportant task or object, it need not be in very great condition. But if that metal is, let's say, gold and has to be used in jewellery, then something much more thorough is required. In this instance a furnace would be necessary with which to burn away and separate out all the impurities. Nothing less will do. Nothing else will produce pure gold.

Likewise the degree of hurt in God's discipline of our lives is an indicator of His plan to make us useful in His service. The more He needs us, the 'hotter' will be the refining in our lives.

If everything in a business is going well, with the productivity and profits graphs heading in the right direction, everyone is satisfied. Sometimes either of these may suddenly tail off and people get anxious. If the trend persists, there must be action: policies are changed; staff may be sacked; procedures are improved; new suppliers are sought, etc. In other words, when things go wrong a halt must be called and a review made in order to make the necessary changes to improve things in the future.

Likewise God may cause our lives to come to a halt so that we reconsider our ambitions, behaviour, relationships, attitudes, etc. Without changes disaster might be round the corner and God wants alterations now so that He can use us so much better in the future.

Eternal Life . . .

The rugby team wasn't exactly composed of top players. In truth, it was just a motley group of people who needed exercise and who were able to give up their Wednesday afternoons for a run-around.

They had one secret weapon — a lad by the name of Brian. He was as broad as he was tall and looked something like a cross between the wrestler Big Daddy and 'BA' from the 'A Team'. When he took his teeth out for the match he looked suitably horrible and terrifying. He was a fierce player, deadly in the scrum since he would make a point of not shaving for the couple of days

before each match! The team's strategy with him was that, if they were anywhere near the opposing team's line, they'd get the ball to Brian and then try and roll him over and over until he could score a try! Sometimes it worked.

Occasionally, Brian's 'enthusiasm' for the game would get the better of him. Rugby is never a gentle sport and the inner goings-on of the scrum are not a pretty sight. On this occasion, Brian, a prop, was having an elbowing, scraping, biting and general gouging session with his opposite number when tempers flared. Suddenly fists were flying and punches were being landed...

Then someone called out: 'C'mon lads — remember it's just a Wednesday afternoon run-around...' and that stopped the fighting. Brian and his opponent growled at each other and plunged back into the scrum.

Why had that message stopped them fighting? It was simply because it made them realise there was nothing worth fighting for. There was nothing at stake in Wednesday afternoon match-es:

— no league or trophy to win;

— no promotion to a better standard.

These matches were simply played for fun.

So, you see, you only fight if there's something worth fighting for.

In 1 Timothy 6:12 Timothy is urged to fight. Literally he's told to 'struggle the good struggle'. He's to strive, to make an effort, to go all out for something.

You only do that if there's something worth fighting for, something worth the struggle. So what is it here?

The something is eternal life. It alone is worth the effort.

The child slipped from a rope and crashed down onto rocks, her head receiving a fearful blow.

Quickly she was rushed to the Accident and Emergency Department of the hospital. There the doctor who examined her was not very interested in her grazed elbow and scraped legs. Nor was he concerned at her untidy appearance and the clothes now grubby from lying on the ground.

He was, however, very concerned about the pain she felt in her head and her frequent vomiting. Immediately he ordered X-rays to be taken of her skull.

Only when those revealed no fracture and it was clear there was nothing more serious than concussion did he take time with some of the minor problems. His first priority had to be to check that the vital parts of the girl's frame were okay. They were essential to life. Other things could wait!

Two thousand years ago people were concerned about money, health, families, homes, jobs and politics. These things had importance.

Paul tells Timothy though that the one thing which really matters is eternal live – see 1 Timothy 6:12. The others may make the few years we have on this earth more comfortable. But first priority must go to finding the new life in Christ which lasts forever. Nothing comes before that.

In the North-east of Scotland, alongside the Moray Firth, lies the little village of Findhorn. Or, at least, there lies the third village to have that name.

The first Findhorn now lies somewhere underneath the waves of the Firth. The second village is buried beneath the nearby Culbin Sands. Very likely both of these were composed of substantial and affluent homes for their time, for it's known that Findhorn in past centuries prospered from trade with the Continent.

No matter how fine these villages looked, they were built in the wrong place. So the first became the victim of a change in the coast-line and the second of exposure to repeated sand movements. Now neither is to be seen.

The fundamental of siting the village correctly was missed and two villages were eventually lost.

The danger for many today is that they are making their lives wonderfully affluent and comfortable. In so many ways they are prospering. None of that, however, is of any use ultimately if the fundamental of gaining eternal life is missed. If life is not 'based' on the solid foundation of faith in Jesus Christ, these other things will perish as surely as did the first two Findhorns.

Evangelism . . .

Modern warfare is very sophisticated. One of the most remarkable innovations has been the heat- seeking missile. All that the attacker has to do is launch his missile in the general direction of the target and it will veer whichever way is necessary, homing in on the quarry.

Likewise, with all our human weakness, our witnessing is always to some degree wide of the mark. By the Spirit, however, God can steer our words until they hit home precisely on the target of the need of the person to whom we speak.

Many years ago a missionary doctor and some others were exploring the African bush in what was then known as Livingstonia. They heard a faint rustling, investigated, and discovered a man, bleeding and torn, for he had stumbled through the mass of thorns in the jungle. He was taken to their hospital where the doctor managed to save his life. He was also found to be blind owing to cataracts. This, too, the doctor operated on and the man's sight was regained. When he was finally fit he left the hospital to return to his own village many miles away.

Some weeks later he returned — 'towing' behind him a human chain of thirty nine other blind people from his village. He'd brought them to the doctor who could give back sight, and every one was treated.

Oh, that we would have a similar determination to bring people to the Doctor who has given 'sight' to us and will do the same miracle for others we find for him.

The successful farmer with large crops and a good income is a man who gets up while it's still dark in the morning and goes to bed long after it's dark at night. In other words, he works very hard for that harvest and he has very little time for other things.

Do we think the Kingdom of God can be established by Christians treating evangelism as a pastime? It's going to cost us to share Christ, and mean long hours with His work as the first priority.

Some children are constantly rebuked, told that they've failed, or that they haven't made the grade expected of them. Child psychologists say that such a child will gradually come to a very deep-seated conclusion that he's not loved or wanted.

Similarly a world which hears only condemnation from Christians will conclude that there's nothing good and no hope or love for them in this 'Christian' message.

A lifeguard at a swimming pool has to give his full attention to what's happening in the water and avoid being distracted. Often young men are used in this job and they tend to be the muscular, bronzed types who make an impression on young ladies who would like to be 'chatted up'. There need be nothing wrong in friendly conversation but if the guard is doing that he may miss someone drowning in the pool. The secondary task of talking to the patrons could distract him from the primary task of saving lives.

Christians find it all too easy to be occupied with talking among themselves on issues which seem so vital at the time but are always secondary to the primary task of winning people into God's Kingdom. Good things can become bad if they distract us from doing what is vital.

The Christian faith clearly was never intended to be the private possession of just the first few disciples.

Sometimes a child will be handed a sweetie by a granny or a neighbour and is told: 'Now don't let the others know — that's just for you.'

The reason granny says that is probably because she hasn't got enough sweets to go round everyone — hence the blessedness of tooth decay is to be kept to just one!

God's grace though is quite sufficient for all who will accept. The 'gospel supply' will not run out if too many come. God loves the whole world and will save all who call on His name.

Therefore the task given to all Christians is to share the good news with all who do not know. 'Go and make disciples of all nations,' said Jesus.

Suppose X's wife is not highly gifted when it comes to cooking.

So, she announces to him and the family: 'I'm sorry dear, but I just don't have the gift of haute cuisine as some do and therefore I cannot cook any more meals. You'll all just have to starve.'

What would X make of that? Would he accept it as a valid argument for his wife never to cook another meal?

I think he'd tell her to get on with it anyway, to do her best...

Let's not argue that we are excused from witnessing on the grounds that some people are specially gifted for that.

In all areas of life, including the spiritual, there are some who are more gifted or especially gifted. But, as with cooking, that does not mean that the rest are excused from the activity. We've all a responsibility to share our faith when we can.

A witness is no more than a person who tells of what has happened in his experience. All Jesus asks you to do is to pass on to others what you know of Him. There is nothing fundamentally difficult about that.

If I asked you to tell me what you know of your parents, your brothers, or your sisters, you wouldn't have to go away and read a book first in order to find out how to tell me. You'd simply open your mouth and pass on the relevant details.

What Jesus asks for are people willing to do that about Him — to tell others who want to know of His love, cross and purpose to change lives, just as He has changed yours.

Witnessing is only a matter of telling what has happened in your own experience.

If you received a court summons to give evidence about someone, or about an incident you had seen, you'd go and do that. You'd have no option and you'd manage.

Jesus has given you a summons to be a witness for Him to this world.

Fear . . .

An article in the magazine 'Time' tells of an incident during the last war when a sergeant was wounded on Guadalcanal. He was hit in the throat by a shell fragment and received seven blood transfusions. In the midst of great pain and anxiety, he wrote a note to his doctor: 'Will I live?'

Back came the reply: 'Yes.'

Another note: 'Will I be able to talk?'

Again the reply: 'Yes.'

Finally the sergeant sent one more note: 'Then what am I worrying about?'

Very often we are anxious in a way which is out of all proportion to the situation we face. It may be bad enough but the things we have in our favour are probably worth far more to us. We need to get a fresh perspective and with that much of our fear would vanish.

Many school children live in fear of the bully in the playground.

Sometimes there's no explanation for why a child is 'picked on' but other times it started when the child somehow wronged the older and stronger boy or girl in some way and the bully won't ever let that incident be forgotten. Perhaps something was spilled one day, perhaps there was a clash of heads in the playground, perhaps a failure to do a job properly. The older child won't let the matter die and takes every opportunity to make life hard and painful for the smaller child.

No amount of apologising changes it and each morning the youngster wonders if this will be the day when he's caught in a corner and given another hammering.

That's how many live in fear concerning God. We wronged Him, perhaps in some very big way years before and now we feel God is passing judgment on us for those sins. Every day seems to bring difficulties and we fear the day when full judgment will fall.

The good news of the gospel, however, is that God 'got even' at the cross. God has no need to punish us, for the full penalty of our sin was laid on Jesus.

Fellowship . . .

The lions who stalk the massive herds of zebras or antelopes on the African plain hunt specially for the lame animal who is being left behind by the others. Cut off from the herd, such an animal is particularly easy prey.

So Satan finds it so very easy to pick on those who become separated from Christian fellowship.

Forgiveness . . .

After you've moved home into a bright, fresh, new house, you don't go back to try and redecorate the old house, to make it look better.

You no longer own that old house. You've left that place behind — it's no longer yours.

So any decorating work that needs done will be in the new house — the place where you are now.

Each day we live now there will be sins in our lives for which we need forgiveness — and that is given. That's the end of it. There's no going back over yesterday's sins.

Besides, there's no time to dwell in the past, for so much needs to be done in the present.

We do not have to wait before being forgiven.

When I was about thirteen I smashed a school piano. Another boy and I thought it would be fun to use the piano as a battering ram on a door. The door won and all sorts of pieces fell off the piano.

Quite hastily I had to appear before the headmaster who had been a good friend to me. He demanded to know how much pocket money I got. I seem to remember it was five shillings a week. I had to pay that amount over to him as a contribution towards the repair of the piano. Only when I did so was that headmaster friendly to me again. There could be no friendship until I had paid at least part of the cost of putting things right.

Now that's how things are in this world.

It's not at all like that though with God. We cannot and need not pay anything for God's friendship.

So many say they cannot become Christians until they prove they can keep up a new lifestyle, or until they've attended church for a while, or until they've put right their past mistakes.

You cannot buy favour with God by any of these methods.

God loves you now, as you are now, and Jesus died for you as you are now. 'While we were still sinners, Christ died for us,' the Bible says (Romans 5:8). That means you can be forgiven the moment you accept Jesus' death for you. There's no waiting, no saving up 'goodness points' to bargain with God.

Genuineness . . .

Someone with an uncontrollable drink problem may finally, in despair, seek help because he's painfully aware of how alcohol has ruined his health, family life and career. He desperately regrets every drink he's had and doesn't ever want to touch another drop. So he appeals to the Samaritans or Alcoholics Anonymous for help.

That's a cry for help coming from real sorrow over failure. There's a genuineness about that. It results in action to bring about a change.

It can be contrasted with a cry for help arising only out of the difficulty caused by a problem.

Someone charged with speeding, or having an excess of alcohol in his blood, may appeal to a top lawyer to plead his case in court. The lawyer will try either to get him off or have the sentence made as small as possible. If his licence were to be suspended, perhaps it would give him serious professional or social difficulties. So he asks the top lawyer to help him.

That kind of asking for help need involve no sorrow at all over what's been done. Indeed the person may go and do exactly the same thing again, this time hoping not to be caught. He has no desire to change, but only wants help to extricate himself from the consequences of his actions.

Only a cry for help of the first type can lead to a sincere conversion. Repentance is not just being sorry. Repentance is being so sorry for offending and hurting a holy and loving God that there's a change of behaviour. That's the cry for help God recognises as genuine.

Giftedness . . .

Imagine that you are setting out on a plane journey and as you go up the steps you notice an 'L' plate stuck to the fuselage. 'Puzzling...' you think to yourself but continue on inside.

Then comes the inevitable pre-flight greeting from the pilot — but this time it's a rather

WWELLLCOME...

nervous, stammering voice which comes over the intercom: 'Welcome ... to my first ffflight... I just want to aaassure yyyou that I've read the manual before coming tttoday ... And I spent a hour in ppprayer as well. Thank you for ffflying with me and I trust your lllife insurance is in good order...

We'll take off soon ... and I just hope we can land again...!'

Now, how would you feel in a situation like that? Would you be comfortable and confident? Would you feel safe? Or, more likely, would you make a quick dash for the exit while there was still time?

It's no wonder churches lack cohesion and members remain unmoved and unmotivated if the people in leadership lack clearly recognised gifts for their work. They might have all the theoretical knowledge possible but if there is no obvious giftedness then no-one will risk following the lead they give and the church will suffer.

It might require only a couple of small batteries to operate a radio or a calculator, but it's no use having only the same power for a washing machine or large size television. A quite different level of power is needed for those.

Likewise God's work needs the gifts of God's wisdom and God's power to get it done. The thinking and methods of the ordinary world simply cannot be transferred over into God's work.

Every year children die because they take little inflated boats or air beds and use them on the sea. These things are fine for the beach or the children's pool but very dangerous on the open sea when a tide can sweep them out and a wave so easily overturn them.

It's obvious some people are clearly not gifted to take responsible positions in church life — 1 Timothy 3 lays out very severe qualifications for leadership and those not fitted had better stay in the shallows. Otherwise they themselves will drown and cause great harm to others in the process.

One day a young man called Joe Soap decided that, rather than be unemployed, he'd become an insurance salesman. He filled out his application form and was then summoned for an interview.

The interviewer explained first of all to Joe that, ideally, they wanted staff who had had some previous experience of this kind of work. Sadly, Joe had no experience at all. He'd never had any job before, so experience was impossible.

'Never mind,' said the interviewer. 'We know everyone can't have experience, so sometimes we're willing to appoint someone because of his qualifications — he'll have a good number of certificates.' Joe had then to explain that he'd never been any good at school, so he had no exam. passes at all.

'Well,' the interviwer still smiled, 'just occasionally we overlook the lack of experience and the absence of qualifications and appoint someone because he has just the right personality to sell insurance.' As they talked, however, it became clear that Joe had no drive in his character. What's more he was shy and found it difficult to talk to people he didn't know well.

Therefore, Joe had no experience, no qualifications and nothing like the right personality. So did he get the job?

Not likely — poor Joe was sent packing. There'd be no job for him.

That's how things work in this world. Jobs go to the right 'types' of people. On that basis, there's no way most of us ought to have been given any job by God.

God, however, does not do things like that, for our skills and background do not form the basis of employment in the Kingdom of Heaven. Instead, our God steps in with His power and His gifts and enables us to do the work to which He calls us.

God's Love . . .

Throughout the Bible we are shown that God wants a very close, personal, loving relationship with His children, an intimacy with us as He had with Jesus.

A father or mother will bend down to a little child, pick him up and hold him close. The child will be comforted when anxious, helped when troubled, encouraged when despondent, guided when unsure and have every need provided.

Our God is doing that to us every day. His heart is open to us, His hand outstretched, in love, and He looks for that love to be returned by us to Him.

Gospel Challenge . . .

Parents know what it's like at meal times...
When the food is ready, everyone is called to the
table. That may take a little time and can involve
more than one calling! Sometimes a little bell
may be rung to get attention. When all else fails,
the parents may opt to 'wring' some necks
instead...!

Finally getting the children to the table doesn't
in itself provide them with adequate nourish-
ment. Any parent can testify that it's one thing to
put food before a child, and another to get him to
eat it. For the child to benefit, he must consume
what is put before him. In some homes that's a
lengthy battle to persuade the child to eat at least
some food. In other homes the opposite applies,
and the statement 'you can leave the table'
means not eating it as well!

Anyway, now we can see the two main elements
in a family's meal-time habits:

— call the family to eat by putting food before
them.

— the latter co-operate by actually eating that
food.

In order for the gospel to benefit any individual, that person must:

— know himself to be called.

— respond by accepting the gospel for himself.

The film 'The Champions' movingly tells the
true story of how top jockey Bob Champion

battles against cancer. From a fit, active, young man, Bob is reduced by the disease to little more than a skeleton, with the inevitable haunted look to his face. With drug treatment, there is just a chance that his life can be saved but the side effects of his chemotherapy are drastic: constant sickness and complete loss of hair are just two. Week after week drags by and his energy and will to conquer the illness are sapped.

The film portrays a time in hospital when Bob is at his lowest ebb. He decides he can go on no longer and makes plans to abandon the treatment and leave the hospital. As he wanders around in despair, he accidentally walks into the children's ward, full of youngsters also battling against cancer. As he sits and watches them, a sweet little girl innocently and realistically asks him: 'Are you going to live, or are you going to die...?' Her words burn into his mind. He pauses but then quietly and firmly replies: 'I'm going to live!'

He made his choice, and live he did.

Likewise each person today needs to choose to accept the offer made to them to live for eternity. Too many fail to face the vital decision that must be made and they just allow their lives to drift away.

Every child at senior school or student at university faces a time when he must choose the subjects on which he will concentrate. In the earliest years of the course it was possible to 'explore the field' but that can't go on forever. The decision faced now is serious — a future career will rest on it. The temptation is to put it off. The day of decision, however, comes and the person must choose.

In more general terms we grow up, learning all the time the range of options and choices available to us in terms of belief, behaviour and ambition. That can't go on forever though as far as Jesus is concerned, for He confronts us with Himself. We've had time to discover the alternatives and now Jesus says: 'I am the way...' (John 14:6). The decision is crucial — not only this life but the next hangs on it. When that day comes — and Jesus says that it's now — there's no avoiding it. We must choose.

If you're driving along a road, searching for the way to go, you may suddenly have that sinking feeling that you've missed your turning. Probably you'll still continue for a little longer, hoping you may yet be right. Gradually, however, you'll be forced to admit to yourself that you've gone wrong.

At that moment there's only one thing to do: turn the car around and head back. If not, you'll simply be going further and further away from your destination.

When we've gone wrong in life that's the only thing to do as well. There's no merit in continuing down the wrong road. We must halt, turn around and start going the way which really will take us where we ought to be.

Perhaps you remember as a youngster trying to

run away from another child. Although you made your little legs pump as fast as they could go, the other child was bigger than you and gradually he got closer and closer to you, until you suddenly felt a hand on your shoulder...

That's the kind of experience many people have with God. For years they've been running but God has gradually been catching up. Now may be the time when at last they sense God has caught them...

Imagine you own a caravan with which you go on holiday, let's say for four weeks a year. Now, on which do you spend most money: the caravan you occupy for four weeks a year, or your main residence in which you live for the other forty eight?

Surely it's on your main home. That must merit far more attention and money, for it has a greater importance when an overall view is taken of the year.

Taking life in its fullest sense, where will we spend most time? Even though we live to be a hundred, that's but a drop in the ocean of eternity. Man lives forever, either in heaven or hell. Therefore it must be the height of folly to spend all our energy and give our whole attention to this life, which is a short excursion, and neglect attending to the matter of eternity.

Can you imagine the stupidity of spending time or money decorating a derelict house which you knew you would shortly have to vacate since it had been served with a demolition order?

Yet the one who strives so hard to satisfy the things of this life, ignoring his future in terms of eternity, is being as foolish as that.

William Barclay, the Scottish theologian, tells of how a visitor was being shown around an art gallery by one of the attendants. In that gallery there were works regarded as masterpieces beyond price. Yet, at the end of the tour, the visitor said: 'Well, I don't think much of your old pictures.'

The attendant answered quietly: 'Sir, I would remind you that these pictures are no longer on trial but those who look at them are.'

All that the man's reaction had done was to show his own blindness to things of real beauty.

Now it's not Jesus who's on trial today. We are the ones who will reveal whether or not we can see what His life, death and resurrection were all worth.

A man was out walking his dog, throwing sticks for her to fetch, with them sometimes landing in a nearby river. The dog was young, only a little more than a puppy and clearly had no real experience of water, yet would fetch the stick from the shallows quite easily.

One throw landed the stick at a point in the river where it was deep right up to the bank. The dog bounded forward eagerly, halted at the edge,

and felt with her paws for the river bed. Of course, this time she couldn't touch the bottom. The stick was only a tantalising yard away and she desperately tried to reach. To catch it, all she had to do was swim a few strokes. She just wouldn't let go of the security of the bank, however, and eventually that stick drifted away downstream and was lost.

How foolish that dog was! Had she but tried, of course the water would have held her up, and she'd have reached her prize. She was unwilling to try and instead lost it.

How often we look longingly for a new life, one of meaning, peace and satisfaction. We even see it in others and we know that it comes from Jesus Christ. But, somehow, though we know we ought to let go, we cling to our old securities. If only we'd let go and trust Him, He'd hold us. But we don't...

Now unless that changes the prize of eternal life will simply drift from us.

A war ends when one side 'surrenders unconditionally'. It accepts the victor's right to dictate terms to it and it ceases all opposition.

Our war with Jesus Christ will end only when we surrender in the same way, when we accept His terms and right over us unconditionally.

All the job adverts or house advertisements in the paper are quite insignificant until one day something catches your eye and you apply for that job or go to view that house. Acting in the situation — doing something about it — makes it important.

Tragically there are many dreamers about Jesus. They're always longing for life to be different — to be more fulfilled — to have fresh purpose and strength — to know themselves forgiven — to overcome some sin.

Until they act, however, in response to Jesus, then dreamers and wishful thinkers are all they'll ever be.

You can go on looking, thinking, considering, making up your mind only for so long about Jesus and then He says: 'Now you must decide about me. You must make up your mind whether you will follow me or not.'

If you're selling a house and an offer comes in, it'll come with a date by which it must be accepted or rejected. You can't opt to put off the decision indefinitely.

If you've been considered for a job, had the interview, and then a letter comes offering you the position, you must decide either way. You can't not decide.

If you've been on the waiting list for membership of a squash club, a golf club, or a social club and the secretary finally writes to tell you your name is at the top of the list, and that you should send in your cheque if you want to go ahead, you must act one way or the other.

If you've been girlfriend, or even boyfriend, to someone for a time and then you receive a proposal of marriage, there has to be a decision.

You see, in the real world we simply have to make decisions and we can't forever put things off.

So, in this real world, Jesus challenges each of us about commitment to Him.

Healing ...

When the victim of a car crash is carried into the Accident and Emergency Department of a large hospital, with bones smashed and internal injuries, the surgeon on duty doesn't reach for the Band Aid. Perhaps there are some superficial cuts which do need that but first there must be radical surgery simply to save the man's life.

Jesus is also a radical surgeon. He does not patch up our lives with sticking plasters when what we need is deeper, more permanent wholeness.

Jesus wants to heal but to heal the whole man. Therefore He begins at the root of the problem and that may very well be a place we would rather He did not go.

There are some who would come gladly today to Jesus for physical healing, for that 'exterior' help to their lives. They won't get it, however, unless Jesus is also allowed to deal with the deeper problems, tensions, frustrations and bad relations as well.

Stress at work, guilt over some sin, a bad relationship in a marriage, fear about the future, refusal of God's will, are just some of the things which can lead to constant headaches, stomach problems, back pain, paralysis, etc.

When that person prays for healing, what long-term good is it for Jesus to remove the pain or disability symptom without also being able to deal with the real cause?

One of the most awkward experiences of my life occurred when giving a slide talk in Motherwell and the projector bulb blew. That was four pounds away, for that's what the bulbs cost.

Thankfully the projector had a second bulb fitted and, asking only for a little patience from my audience, within a few seconds I was able to slide a switch and the second bulb lit up.

After about two minutes that one blew as well. Another four pounds gone!

I hadn't had the Scout motto: 'Be prepared' drummed into me for nothing: I had a third bulb in my pocket! The congregation sang a chorus, while I unscrewed the relevant compartment, inserted the new bulb and off we went again. That bulb lasted all of thirty seconds. Everyone smiled—I prayed the earth would swallow me up — and thankfully someone fetched another projector.

When I got home I examined the projector I'd been using. Someone, somehow, had set the voltage switch to one hundred and ten volts instead of two hundred and forty. That was enough to upset these delicate and expensive bulbs and to keep blowing them. When that was put right, no more bulbs ever blew as long as the projector was in my possession.

To simply keep replacing the projector bulbs was futile. Something more fundamental was wrong and that was what had to be put right to make it useful.

Likewise Jesus wants to heal the whole man.

Imagine going to the doctor and saying: 'Oh, doctor, I've got such a headache...,' and — instead of examining you — he looks straight at your head and says: 'Headache, how dare you do this? I rebuke you. I tell you off. Don't do this any more!'

That's not an approach to treatment taught in too many medical schools and I think most of us would be rather taken aback by such an approach from our GP.

Yet, that is precisely what Jesus did with respect to the fever of Peter's mother-in-law — see Luke 4:39.

Jesus warned the fever off, and it went away, and she was well. That approach leaves the impression that, in this instance, the illness had a demonic connection.

Holy Spirit . . .

One sport most would never want to try is ski-jumping. There is nothing in us that could possibly want to come thundering down a ninety metre hill and launch ourselves into outer space...

Why not?

a) Because we couldn't ski well enough to reach even the bottom of the launching slope.

b) Because we have no particular love of heights.

c) Because we're not amongst that group of people who think it's fun to risk their lives!

So, there's no way that, even if the opportunity was given to us on a plate, we would try such a sport. We're the wrong kind of people for that.

The first disciples must have listened to Jesus as He detailed His plans for them to walk in His footsteps, do His deeds, carry on His work and they must have thought to themselves: 'Oh no, we're just the wrong kind of people for that...'

Before they had time to run, however, Jesus told them: 'You will receive power...' (Acts 1:8) and He went on to speak of the Holy Spirit.

In other words, if we were not cowardly Scots (or whatever), but instead somehow had the temperament and the ability of one of these daredevil Finns, Austrians or Norwegians, then we would go out there and jump over one hundred metres and win the title.

If some kind of transfusion could replace our watery blood with their sterner stuff, then we'd have a go and do it, overcoming all fear.

Jesus' message to these disciples is like that.

Whoever said the work of God's Kingdom was going to be done in the strength and power of man?

It was always God's plan to give His people His Spirit to do His work.

Perhaps many years ago some of you owned a moped. That is, in the days when a moped actually had pedals (modern ones don't usually have them).

Did the fact that it had pedals mean that those were what you used to get yourself along the road while riding that bike?

Of course not. Once moving, the pedals were there only as footrests, because by then the engine had roared into life, and you travelled by its power, not your own.

Don't be the kind of Christian who's like a moped rider who's constantly pedalling. You have an engine — the power of the Spirit has been given to you.

Do you ever have the experience of continually meeting the same person? Sometimes it seems that wherever you go, there he is also...

As you read Acts, that's how it is with the Holy Spirit. He's there on every page — you just can't avoid Him. He's the key figure in the book.

In a war, the side which wins is the one with the superior weapons and superior fighting skills.

Likewise the Holy Spirit within the Christian will always bring forth greater gifts and skills than anything the devil can inspire in his forces. See 1 John 4:4.

Some people doubt God's willingness to use them, as if He would withhold the power of His Spirit from their lives.

In Acts 1:4 Jesus described the coming of the Spirit to the disciples as receiving the 'gift' which the Father had promised. That choice of word helps us here in two ways:

1) When a gift is being passed on, the greater amount of work is done by the giver. At birthdays or Christmas, when children are receiving presents, the effort of unwrapping a gift is very little compared to choosing and preparing it. That work has been done by the father or mother who considered the child's needs, scoured the shops for the right thing, wrapped it up beautifully and finally presented it to the child.

2) Because it is a gift, the child did not earn it. Therefore — in a sense — he can't fail to get it. In fact, the only way he could miss out on the gift is by refusing it. Since children know that parents love them and will only give something good, they're never likely to turn a gift down!

So:

1) Passing on the gift of the Spirit is God's work. It depends on His action, not on ours.

2) God will give the gift to every one of His children. No-one will be without power unless

he spurns what God wants to give.

It was picnic time in the village park and it seemed everyone had come. One of the busiest local stores had organised the picnic and everyone who shopped there regularly was entitled to have their family at the picnic. There had been games, races and special displays, but now it was time to pass out food parcels.

One little boy just stood by and watched, afraid to join the line of children waiting to get a parcel. At his age he didn't know if his family were on the list that allowed them to be there. So he wasn't sure if he qualified for a food parcel or not.

The little boy was afraid that when he got to the head of the queue he would be turned away empty handed. Rather than have that happen to him, he opted just to watch.

Many would seek the power of God's Spirit if only they could be sure they would receive, but they're afraid they'll come away empty handed. Yet there's no need for any fear, for the promise of the gift of the Spirit is for every child of God. Every Christian qualifies.

In Luke 11:13 Jesus instructs disciples to 'ask' God the Father for the Holy Spirit. If Jesus thought it necessary to teach that, why do many Christians assume that there is nothing for them to do with regard to receiving the Spirit?

Most car engines have a 'choke', a flap attached

to the carburettor, to help the engine start when cold. Some chokes are automatic and some manual.

If there's a choke knob on the dashboard, then the driver knows immediately that it's manual and he must pull it to make the choke work. If there's no such lever, then it's automatic. Obviously, no manufacturer would provide a knob with an automatic choke, for it would serve no purpose.

So, it would be nonsense for Jesus to command Christians to ask for the Spirit if He meant them to do nothing, if everything about the Spirit were automatic. Why tell them to ask if they have no part to play in receiving the Spirit?

To divide Christ and the Spirit is to attempt to sever the Trinity and is a nonsense.

Joe and Jean are brother and sister. Jean falls in love with Jim, who is her cousin and marries him.

Joe has always hated cousins but Jim is now his brother-in-law as well as his cousin. So, when Jean and Jim visit Joe, Joe can't refuse Jim entry on the grounds that he is his cousin without simultaneously refusing his brother-in-law, for Jim is both. So, Joe tells Jim to come in and thereby is host to his brother-in-law and his cousin.

Simple...isn't it?

Invite Christ in and the Spirit must be there as well, for they are one.

Inconsistency . . .

Sometimes you will see a golfer whose shots take him from one side of the fairway to the other, often landing in the rough at the edge. It may take him several swipes to extricate himself from one spot, only for him to fly the ball right across the course to another problem area on the other side. A great deal of frenzied hacking follows and any progress towards the actual hole is painfully slow.

For many people life is full of drama but very little solid progress. They stagger from one crisis to another. With great excitement they move from one situation off into a new direction, only quickly to find themselves in yet more trouble. Much energy goes into removing them from that problem, only for the pattern to keep repeating... Oh for a little calm, careful thought and a proper alignment of that life with the target!

Jesus' Baptism . . .

The closeness of Father to Son is revealed verbally by God at Jesus' baptism. After He comes out of the water, the heavens open and the Spirit comes down and rests on Him and God says: 'You are my Son, whom I love; with you I am well pleased.' (Mark 1:11).

When a man first sees a child of his come into the world, he just has to tell others. Usually there are 'phone calls to relatives and the neighbours also must be told early on. Apart from the formal passing on of the details, usually his great news will also be brought up in conversations with total strangers. He'll find himself telling the postman, the milkman, the assistant at the corner shop, the waitress in a restaurant, the office cleaner and so on. It's as if he just can't keep such good news to himself! He can't keep it quiet!

Also it's as if God just had to tell the world of His delight in His child... It's as if He couldn't keep it quiet!

Judgment...

Imagine sailors who by their own carelessness and poor seamanship run their ship aground on rocks and are stranded with the seas gradually pounding their vessel to pieces. Imagine then, the even greater folly if they refuse rescue from the lifeboat which sails to their aid. So, have they anyone to blame but themselves when, some hours later, they at last realise they will drown? Their plight, and the fact that it continues, is of their own making.

Likewise those who run their lives aground, and then refuse salvation from Jesus, have only themselves to blame when, on Judgment Day, they realise their destiny. Theirs was the double sin of initial disobedience compounded by refusing the opportunity of rescue.

Love . . .

A wall built only of single brick is really quite thin and superficially doesn't look very robust. Yes, of course, it has foundations but even so, one brick on top of another is quite a balancing act. We would expect it to fall over at the first nudge.

The fact that it doesn't is entirely due to the cement which joins each brick to the next. Without that, the slightest gust or push would bring the lot tumbling down. With it, however, it is safe and can stand very strong winds, or even all the neighbourhood children clambering over it!

What cement is to a wall, so love is to Christians. (See John 13:34-35)

With it we can stand firm in the midst of this troubled world. Without it we come crashing down in a terrible heap of disaster.

Anyone who has seen the result of a gas explosion will never take the stability of a building for granted. A house can look perfectly secure — a solid, stable structure. In seconds though it can be demolished to no more than a heap of rubble.

Likewise constant arguments, disagreements, jealousies and bitterness between Christians are explosive material, capable of destroying any church. We need the cement of love to hold us together.

Mercy . . .

Aberdeen, in Scotland, is known as the granite city, and much of that tough rock was hewn from Rubislaw Quarry, which lies within the city boundary. The quarry is little more than a vast hole in the ground, four hundred and eighty feet deep, nine hundred feet long and seven hundred and fifty feet wide, the result of removing tons of rock to build the city over the last century and a half. It's now closed and disused, but in the days when it was a working quarry visitors were welcome.

Those visitors certainly required stout hearts, for viewing the quarry was a terrifying and exhilarating experience. The quarry, naturally, had a high fence around the edge to prevent accidents, but, in order to allow visitors to gaze down into the depths of the earth, at one place there was a small platform built out over the edge. There they stood, clinging on firmly and peering over the rail to see tiny figures scurrying around at the bottom of the quarry, breaking up the granite to take it to the surface. Hearts raced as people looked down into this great abyss, all too aware that only that secure platform stopped them falling to their deaths.

God's mercy holds us up like that platform. A hand of love has reached out and caught us on our fall into hell. Accept that mercy and you are safe, held fast by a loving Father. Refuse it and your fall continues, a fall to eternal death.

Newness . . .

When it was first invented, the Sinclair ZX81 computer was a marvel. Even with just 1K of memory, people were impressed at what it could do.

No matter how much affection some may still have for their very first computer, a ZX81 is no use today to run some of the more sophisticated programs, whether databases, spreadsheets, or word processing. It's just not adequate for what's needed now.

In Jesus God burst right through the old forms with a revelation and a salvation which is so great and far reaching.

Now, the whole world is offered the gospel, not just the people of one land. Every man has direct access to God and he doesn't have to offer repeated sacrifices through priests based in a temple at Jerusalem.

The old wineskin wouldn't do for the new wine of the gospel.

Obedience . . .

When a managing director 'phones through to the junior clerk and says: 'I want you in my office now,' can you imagine the junior clerk replying: 'I'm very sorry, but you'll just have to wait. It doesn't suit me to come at the moment'?

Bosses don't wait!

So, the Lord God Almighty is not to be kept waiting either until His commands suit our convenience.

A typical tea-time scenario in many a home goes something like this.

Tea is virtually ready and so father is sent to summon the children downstairs from playing in their bedroom. 'Tea's ready...,' he calls upstairs. 'Coming!' is the reply.

Five minutes later no-one has appeared. So again he calls, this time a little more insistently: 'Tea's ready. Get downstairs.' 'Coming!' chimes a little voice.

Another five minutes elapse and still no children. Father shouts: 'Now come on. Tea is on the table.' Again the answer, 'Coming!'

After another two minutes, a final shout, a final reply of 'Coming!' and up the stair father marches, saying sternly, 'Stop coming, and come!'

Many have heard God's word of command so many times and keep promising to do what He says, but the time to put that into practice never

81

quite arrives. To such people, God's word now is: 'Stop coming, and come!'

Often we tone down the commands of Jesus until they become acceptable.

We don't keep wild animals in our homes, but a dog, cat, hamsters, goldfish, budgies, etc. — all these are kept by man.

What's the difference?

The difference is that there are some animals we can't tame, and so it would disrupt our lives unacceptably to have them close to us. The others though have been 'domesticated' by man — i.e., made to conform to a pattern we like and find acceptable. Hence they become our pets.

Something like that is what we've done with many commands of Jesus. We preach them and acknowledge them as foundational for all Christians. But we've tamed them — softened their impact until we can live with them.

Many hear only what they think they should hear.

The classic case of that is when someone asks: 'Good morning, how are you?' and you reply, 'Well, I'm really feeling terrible today,' and they don't pick up the negative response, but simply go on with 'Fine, fine...'

Very often we hear what we think we should hear. We're deaf to what we don't expect to hear, or don't want to hear.

That's true in ordinary conversations — it's

true also when God tries to impress His will on us.

Sometimes we are so unwilling to do what God asks of us that we try very hard to persuade God that His choice of us is wrong.

That's like someone being offered a job and telling the employer he must be crazy because he comes from the worst housing scheme in the city, from the worst school in that housing scheme, and that he's the very poorest pupil in that worst school.

No-one surely would give that response to a prospective employer, telling him he's making a mistake.

Yet, we think we can tell God His business when we opt out of what He shows He wants us to do for Him.

83

Persecution . . .

Imagine a boss warning a disobedient young employee about the way he does his work, only to find that by the next month the man's behaviour is worse. He summons him and, instead of receiving an apology, the boss is told that he's been running the company wrongly all these years, that the business will fail if that continues and that the young man has every intention of carrying on doing his work his way no matter what the boss says!

How would the boss feel about that? Wouldn't he be furious?

Without wishing to carry over connotations of being rude, essentially our stand for Christ conveys a message to the world like that of the young employee to his boss. When we stand up for Christian principles, we are at least implicitly rejecting theirs. We are saying that their ways are not right or acceptable. It's not so surprising then that the world hits back at Christians.

Let's say your next door neighbour has a little boy who's rather wild. One day you see him out on his bicycle and as you watch you see him riding his bike down the wrong side of the road — he's heading towards the oncoming traffic.

Well, that's serious, and out of concern you try and correct him. What he's done is not personally offensive or damaging to you but there's still a need to put him right.

The next day the lad is out on his bike again and this time you see him taking a short-cut and riding his bike right through your garden, destroying ten prize rose bushes on his way. Out you go, thoroughly mad, rant and rave at him for a while and then go to his parents to take your complaint further.

Why is your reaction more extreme this time? Because this time his actions are directly damaging to you.

So, the world isn't much bothered about Christians whose lives don't affect them. Stand against the world in some way, however, damage someone's selfish interests and there will be a sharp retaliation. The whole reaction of the Pharisees and Sadducees to Jesus is an instance of this. Acts 16:16-24 and 19:23-34 would be other good biblical examples.

Anyone in employment knows the terrible tension which exists when on probation in the job — i.e., if you know someone's watching how you do your work and looking for any faults. That creates a lot of pressure for the employee.

Sometimes he can begin to feel that the boss wants to find fault, that he's looking for an excuse for a dismissal. Then there is an almost unbearable strain under which to work.

That is what Jesus had to live with for almost three years. He was plagued in His ministry by those who followed Him around, constantly trying to find fault, looking for a reason to accuse Him.

No Christian has a guarantee that life will be any easier.

When a golfer's shot is blocked by trees, he faces a situation which is not only difficult but dangerous. The difficulty is obvious — somehow the ball has to get past those trees. The danger is when it doesn't!

For when a golf ball strikes a tree, it might as well have hit something made of rubber, because it will ricochet off at enormous speed. The player strikes his shot with great force — and immediately it is thrown back at him. So, if he's not quick to duck, his own action in hitting the ball can cause him injury.

As the early church moved forward with God, something similar happened to it. The more the Christians advanced the gospel, the more force was used against them in response by those who wanted to block its path.

So today, whenever God's Word is truly presented in the power of the Spirit, there is opposition, and some of it can hurt!

We have a tendency to think that trouble will stay away providing we're doing what God wants and especially if God is clearly with us and blessing our efforts for Him.

That's like a driver thinking that, providing he keeps precisely to the Highway Code, he'll never have an accident.

Such a driver always signals carefully, checks his mirror, never overtakes on a corner and keeps within the speed limit even when he's late for an appointment... So, he thinks he shouldn't ever have an accident. He's doing everything right. It wouldn't be fair for there to be a problem.

Life though isn't always fair and accidents do happen, even to careful drivers. No-one can guard against all circumstances and, especially, there are other drivers who are not so careful..!

So, unfair though it may seem, God's servants are still persecuted. We're in spiritual warfare against the devil and there's nothing fair in war.

Pharisees . . .

The name 'Pharisee' means 'The Separated One' and they had separated themselves from ordinary men and ordinary lives in order to keep every last detail of the Jewish law. To be sure they did that, they 'put a hedge about the law' — i.e., because they considered it would be terrible to break even a small point of the law, they did far more than the law required in order to be on the safe side.

If a shopkeeper wants to be scrupulously honest and never cheat anyone when he weighs something out on his scales he'll always give the customer a little more than the precise amount. 'After all,' he'll reckon to himself, 'my scales might not be adjusted perfectly, so I must make an extra allowance.'

Now that's how the Pharisees behaved with respect to the law. They worried that they might fall short in any way and so they left a margin of safety by always doing more than the law required.

Prayer . . .

From time to time in the correspondence columns of local papers a letter will appear to thank an unknown hero. Someone's child has been rescued from a river, or his mother picked up after falling in the street, or his wife dragged from a blazing car. The helper has done what was needful at the time but then disappeared immediately and now no-one knows who he or she was — an unknown support and help.

Don't most of us owe an inestimable amount to our unknown supports and helps — to those who have prayed for us at times of difficulty? No-one asked them to do it and we weren't even aware at the time and yet our survival was because of their prayers.

If your car breaks down in a serious way and you manage to get it to a garage you'll say to the people there: 'Fix it.' That's reasonable. They are the trained mechanics. They know how the car works. You don't, at least not to the degree necessary for a major repair. They are the experts and you expect them to put the vehicle right for you.

So, it's not unreasonable for us to ask the omnipotent and merciful God to intervene on behalf of His people, to come to their aid. He is both able and willing to do what they cannot.

Preaching . . .

The preacher's job is like that of the wholesaler in commerce. The wholesaler markets goods to his customer (the shopkeeper) but not just that. For before he can sell anything he must first get his supplies from the manufacturer. Thus he is a middleman in business, in two directions: a) receiving goods from the makers; b) then passing them on to the shopkeeper.

Likewise the preacher is in business in two directions. By prayer and careful study he receives his message from the Creator and then passes that on to his audience or congregation.

Priorities . . .

Out of all the things you have to do, what always gets done and what is usually left because you never get round to it?

The answer reveals what things are real priorities.

Sometimes you'll find someone who's an extremely busy person, on the go morning to night, but there's just one TV programme he never misses. Or, perhaps, it's going to support his local football team once a week that's vital. Yet, because he's so 'busy', there are jobs around the house that never get done, or someone who never gets visited.

The truth is that we can all find time for what we really want to do.

So, what's undone and what's never missed no matter the circumstances...?

How tragic if things like prayer, worship, Bible study and Christian service come under the heading of the things usually left undone. That would surely reveal that God has a very low priority in your life.

Purity . . .

One popular advert. for washing powder involves a housewife taking a newly washed garment and holding it up in front of a window through which the sun is streaming. 'Can it stand such a test?' is the question being asked of the washing powder, or will the light reveal that some deep stains still remain?

Christians' lives have to be able to stand such a test, the test of being in God's light. In Philippians 1:10 Paul says we are to be 'pure' — the Greek word used is eilikrinēs which combines the words for sunshine and testing. Hence the Christian is so to live that his life is capable of being tested like a garment being held up to the light without any stain appearing.

A common reason for a car to break down is because of a blocked fuel filter. Dirt from the petrol has covered the filter and now the fuel won't pass through. That filter has to be cleaned before the engine will go again. It has to be able to let the fuel flow through.

So, we must live in such a way that we are channels for God's Spirit. Get rid of the things you know are wrong, anything which brings a blockage.

One of the challenges shoe manufacturers have

to face is the fact that every day our feet lose the equivalent of half a cupful of perspiration! That's a lot of moisture. If we're not to go around with wet feet all the time, they have to design shoes in such a way that the perspiration can evaporate out but other water cannot come in!

Similarly the challenge each Christian has to face is that he must allow God's Spirit out through him to affect this world but not allow the world's spirit to come in and damage his life.

Purpose . . .

A man retired from a senior position in business moved to live in a new area. Now all purpose had gone out of life. He became broody and depressed, worried about the least thing. Illness was never far away either, and he seemed to be ageing fast.

Then, acting on someone's advice, he plunged himself into community activity. He quickly discovered that the skills he'd learned over many years in commerce were precisely those needed to lead one group, advise another, manage the books of some other body. Before long he had a more active life than when he had been working.

That man became fitter, healthier and happier than most men half his age. In fact, he outlived most of his former colleagues, eventually dying in his nineties. He had vision and purpose for life and that made him fruitful.

God calls His people to be active for Him by giving them vision and purpose, as they are commanded to 'be witnesses in Jerusalem, Judea, Samaria and to the ends of the earth.' (Acts 1:8)

At university I often felt the pressure of being told that it was a privilege to be there, that this was a unique opportunity and that I ought not to squander it. So, from time to time that spurred me to do some work and try to pass my exams.

Not everyone responded like that. Some

seemed to feel they were at university principally to drink coffee by day and beer by night, and organise radical new political societies. I reckon something of the privilege of education was lost on them!

They would be the ones who handed exam. papers in just ten minutes after the exam. had begun — they had nothing to write. You see, they had a great opportunity, but they squandered it. They 'blew it'.

God says to his church: 'See, I have placed before you an open door that no-one can shut...' (Revelation 3:8). The opportunity is there for Christians to step out in faith and advance the Kingdom of God. That, however, will take determination and single-mindedness. We can't be distracted by peripheral activities or we will have squandered our opportunity.

What really matters to you? What are you giving your life for? What are you spending your time and your energy on?

Is it worth it? Is it right? Will it last?

As a child I loved to chase soap bubbles as they floated through the air, catching them if they didn't float too high. Of course, there was never much of a reward for my effort for as soon as I caught a bubble it 'popped' and disappeared.

Don't spend your life chasing things as empty as those soap bubbles, things which just come to nothing in your fingers as soon as you reach them.

Real Life . . .

To dig up buried treasure you must have a good map. Digging in the wrong location won't get you anywhere except to the point of exhaustion. The treasure is only in one place — you must dig there if you are to find it.

Those who pursue real happiness in life had better be sure likewise that they are looking in the right place — nothing but disappointment will result from searching elsewhere. God's 'map', the Bible, tells us many times where the one, right place is — it's in Jesus (e.g., John 14:6; Acts 4:12).

Resurrection . . .

When someone dies, a son or daughter may assert that the deceased's last wish was to leave all his money to him or her: an important assertion with far-reaching implications, not only for that individual but perhaps also for many others. No-one, however, can be expected to pay any heed to such a claim unless the person can produce evidence to back up the statement — normally a will by the deceased putting the matter in writing. A statement is useless unless there is evidence to validate it.

Likewise, in 1 Corinthians 15 it would have been useless for Paul simply to have baldly stated that Jesus rose from the dead. By itself, such an assertion (in v.4) could simply have been the subject of mockery. In fact, he is able to go on (in verses 5 to 8) and list a whole series of witnesses who saw the risen Jesus — the evidence he needs to validate his claim.

Near the end of Jules Verne's book 'Round the World in Eighty Days' there is a dramatic episode when the adventurers are desperately hurrying back to Britain from America. To everyone's horror, the ship runs out of coal to fire the boilers. Instantly the order is given to start pulling apart the superstructure of the vessel — wooden railings, furniture, deck boards and so on. Finally they just make it to land, but by this time there is little left other than a hull, boiler and funnel. Yet,

of course, they had to have at least that. They
simply couldn't dispense with these, otherwise
the ship would have gone down.

In 1 Corinthians 15 Paul tells doubters in
Corinth a similar message (in verses 17 and 18):
'Dispense with the resurrection and you've
nothing left — your faith will sink.' Christianity
cannot exist if the resurrection of Jesus did not
really happen.

Imagine you live in a land where there is a
terrible, fierce, enormous, fire-breathing dragon.
All the citizens are terrified and try to hide,
however, this dragon has finely developed senses
of hearing, smell and of sight, and one by one he is
finding and eating them! No-one escapes and
gradually the whole population is being deci-
mated.

Then, one day, on to the scene comes a knight
in shining armour — it's St George! And —
hurray! — he's come to fight the dragon.

Pessimism, however, abounds among those
who remain. 'You've no hope,' all the people say.
'You'll just be eaten too...'

Brave St George is not put off though and while
the people watch from a safe distance, out he
strides to fight the dreaded beast. The dragon
snorts and licks his charred lips at the thought of
this lightly grilled morsel for supper.

The fight begins. The dragon breathes fire,
thrashes his pointed tail and bites fiercely. St
George responds by cutting and thrusting with
sword and spear.

On the battle rages and, as they fight, gradually

they move behind a hill, out of sight of the people, although they can still hear the sound of fighting.

Suddenly, all is silent. They know the battle is over, and so the people wait. Who's going to appear from behind the hill?

Will it be the dragon? If so, then St George is dead — eaten up — and the people will live knowing that one day they in turn will become the dreaded enemy's food.

What's this?! It's St George. He lives! Therefore it's the dragon who's perished and the people know that at last they're free.

So Jesus, having suffered on the cross for our sins, then went into direct battle with Satan's

most powerful weapon and our greatest enemy — death. Death thought it had another easy victim but that fight raged right on until the third day. Then the fight was over and it was Jesus who appeared. He had triumphed over death and now those who belong to him need no longer fear the old foe (1 Corinthians 15:55-57).

When the first Americans stepped on to the moon's surface, they uttered the words: 'One small step for man — one giant leap for mankind.' One of the reasons those words were spoken was Neil Armstrong's consciousness that landing on the moon was not something he had done just for himself but on behalf of mankind in general. He was the first to go where many others would follow.

So Jesus' resurrection from death is the first of many who will follow likewise. See 1 Corinthians 15:20-23.

Many clubs — sporting, social, community — are private. Only members can enter. Yet it is still usually possible to get in by one method and that is to be taken by a member. Providing you 'belong' to someone who is entitled to entry, then you enjoy the same privileges.

Likewise our passage from this life, through death, and on to resurrection is possible only if we belong to Jesus. See 1 Corinthians 15:23.

Sacrifice . . .

In Glenmoriston, in the Highlands of Scotland, there is a cairn in memory of Roderick Mackenzie who allowed his captors to think he was Prince Charles Edward Stuart (Bonnie Prince Charlie) and who accepted execution in order to enable his leader to escape. He never needed to die like that. At any time he could have saved himself but he valued his prince's life above his own and so accepted death in his place.

Jesus similarly took our place to allow us to escape the death which should have been ours. He valued our lives above His own.

Security . . .

The three-year-old was secure in his father's arms, as Dad stood in the middle of the swimming pool. Dad though decided to tease the child and began to walk slowly down the pool, gently chanting 'Deeper...and deeper...and deeper' as the water rose higher and higher. The small lad's face registered increasing degrees of panic and he held all the more tightly to his father, who, thankfully, could easily touch the bottom.

Yet, had the little boy been able to analyse his situation, he'd have realised that there was no reason for any increased anxiety. For in that particular swimming pool, the depth of water even at the shallowest end would have gone over his head. Therefore, whether he was there or at the deepest point made no difference. If at any time he'd not been held up, he'd have drowned. No matter where he was in the pool, his safety always depended on Dad.

At some times in life, all of us feel we're getting 'out of our depth': problems abound, there's a sudden bereavement, a job is lost, a financial crisis strikes, etc. The temptation is to panic, for we feel we've lost control. Yet, as with the child in the swimming pool, the truth is that we never had control over the most valuable things of life. We've always been held up by the grace of God, our Father, and that will not change now. He's not out of His depth and therefore we're as safe now as ever we've been.

Service . . .

How willing are you to have your 'right' to peace and quiet taken away in order to help someone else?

If it's a quarter past three on a Friday and you suddenly realise you have no money, you can make it to a bank in time and draw some out. But if it's a quarter to four, you're too late (at least at most banks), because closing time is half past. You're stuck until Monday morning.

There are hours for business and if you don't call during those, then that's your hard lines.

That may be acceptable business practice, but is it an acceptable way for Christians to care for people? Is that the laying down of your will, your life, as Jesus said would be done by his disciples?

Sometimes we all build 'walls' around ourselves — systems to protect ourselves from others. We may need these up to a point, but then they take over and others cannot get help from us unless their need or problems happen to coincide with our availability.

That's not a lot like Jesus. Jesus did not teach us to 'love our own lives' but to lose them for his sake.

Sin-cleansing . . .

You climb into your bath dirty. When you get out, where's the dirt? Round the rim of the bath for the next four weeks!

You leave the dirt behind. The act of washing makes you physically clean.

The person who comes to Christ is made clean spiritually. The sin is left behind. It is gone from his life. A visible expression of this is in baptism.

Sin's Grip . . .

I was walking through a park and passed a massive oak tree. Of all trees, the oak seems to give the impression of immense strength and solidity. On this occasion though my eye was caught by something else. Right alongside the trunk of the tree, a vine had grown up.

At first it must have been rather small — nothing to bother about, but over the years it had become taller and taller. As time passed, its branches, its creepers, had wound themselves around and around the branches of the oak tree. By the time I passed, the whole of the lower half of the tree was covered by the vine and no leaves grew there. So thick was the mass of small feelers, it looked as though the tree had innumerable birds' nests on it. Now, of course, the tree was in danger, for it was gradually being enveloped by the vine and its life was being squeezed from it. It was being taken over — eventually it would die.

The gardeners in that park, however, had seen the danger and done something about it. With a saw they had simply severed the trunk of the vine — one neat cut right across the middle. So on the day I passed, all the mass of the vine's branches were still there on the oak — the appearance of having its grip on the tree was still there. The reality now was that the vine's power was broken. It was dead, and the truth of that would gradually become plain as the weeks and months passed and the creepers began to lose their grip and fall away from the tree.

Here we see:

1) How easy it is for sin, which begins so small and seemingly insignificant, to grow in its power over our lives, until it has a grip which is strangling us.

2) How Christ's death has slain sin in the believer's life. Oh yes, the 'creepers' of sin will still be there and have some effect, but the power is broken and gradually our lives should be reflecting that victory of Christ for us.

Sin's Spread . . .

In spring time plants shoot up in the garden. Many of these are welcome as bulbs come to life, but, sure as anything, there'll also be weeds.

Perhaps early on there won't be many, only one or two. Just ignore them — there aren't many and they're not very big right now. Don't bother about them.

Then when mid-summer comes, what will you find? Will they have gone away by themselves?

No — indeed, you'll discover they've spread and by now they're choking the life out of all the plants which you want to grow in the garden. You ought to have plucked out the weeds when they first appeared.

It also seems impossible to prevent any 'weeds' appearing in our lives — those seemingly small, wrong thoughts and apparently insignificant, minor misdeeds. The temptation is to leave them alone — to ignore them, perhaps hoping they'll just go away. That, however, never happens, and without repentance and action to avoid such behaviour in future these things will grow in our lives, and the good we want is choked out.

Spiritual Warfare...

Almost any football team will have one: the strapping six-footer, muscles bulging, immaculately turned out in impeccably ironed shirt and shorts, with boots gleaming and not a trace of mud from the last game. Such a player is sure to strike dread into the hearts of the opposition as they see him trot on to the field of play. They'll probably set their strongest player to 'mark' him, to pay him close attention, lest he run loose and score many goals.

Very frequently though this fine-looking player cannot match his appearance with skill. He may look the perfect athlete but yet be clumsy, always in the wrong place and unable to control the ball if it comes his way. When that's the case, the opposing team will quickly stop giving him any special attention. They're not going to waste good manpower on someone who's no threat to them.

Also Satan is not impressed by Christians or by a church which just looks good. He doesn't mind how nice/attractive our buildings are, how well we dress, how many meetings we hold, how expensive our Bibles are. None of these outward things may mean anything. Yet let the most humble of Christians or churches really begin to attack the kingdom of darkness and Satan will respond with the fiercest of opposition. Could it be that, if we experience little or no spiritual battle, our discipleship to Christ is mostly only surface deep?

During a war, troops can find a measure of peace and even safety sheltering in trenches or dug-outs, keeping their heads down. Wars though are not won by staying there, and if there is to be any advance at all then they must get up and out of their trenches and fight. As soon as they do that there'll be all the chaos and bloodshed of battle. That's warfare, and tranquility will have gone.

Sometimes Christians look forward naively to a time when numbers will be increasing, worship is good, people are being cared for, God's presence is being sensed and so on. They imagine that to be wonderfully peaceful and serene — an idyllic time for Christians. But these good things only come when Christians get out of their trenches and are serious about being Christ's disciples — and that always means warfare, and it's hard, difficult and demanding.

When you are at work for God, pray constantly for the protection of your loved ones.

Those who give information to the police — 'supergrasses' — have to get police protection for their families. Otherwise, a wife, a child, a parent could become the victim of blackmail or retribution.

That can happen in spiritual warfare too. Satan can try to prevent us serving God, or simply try to hit back at us, by assaulting our families. He doesn't accept our definitions of fairness and will use any means he can to stop us.

Stubbornness . . .

Boys will often play with bows and arrows. In its simplest form that means finding a springy length of young wood, bending it to shape and then tying string to each end.

When the game is finished, sometimes these bows lie around discarded for a long time. If, later, the string is removed, the wood never goes straight again.

It had been held in that bent shape for such a time that it doesn't recover the straightness it had originally.

So, we can bend and distort our lives for so long, resisting God so firmly, that it becomes virtually impossible to straighten out again. We become immune to God's voice pleading with us, our consciences get hardened and we are confirmed in our disobedience. It's not that God gives up — rather that we just get used to things as they are and, the shape of our lives stays wrong.

Most of us will have had the experience of hearing the 'phone ring, picking up the receiver, instantly recognising the voice of the caller...and thinking, 'I wish I'd been out!' That's the last person you wanted to speak to at that time. What has happened is that the caller has 'phoned to ask about something you ought to have done by then but in fact you haven't even started on it.

Very often we talk as though we want God to

speak to us but the truth is that we'd really prefer if He didn't 'call' us about many matters. We'd feel too awkward to be asked about these promises we once made! So, in a sense, most of the time our spiritual phone is 'off the hook' as far as God's concerned.

Submission . . .

We're tempted to limit God to the ways we think acceptable:
— His presence to the confines of a church building;
— His ways of doing things to our traditions.

We tend to reject some things as not being from God when they don't fit with the way we were brought up, or if they lie outside of our experience or control. We feel a need to defend ourselves from them.

Any time I have seen a lion, there have always been thick metal bars between it and me, either at the circus or zoo. The reason the animal is caged, of course, is because otherwise it could escape and do things we wouldn't want...like eating people!

So we keep lions caged.

That's right with lions but dare we ever try to do that with God? Should we shut Him away? Are we to defend ourselves from what God might do?

What kind of relationship exists where the so-called disciples dictate to the Master what He can or cannot do among them?

Can God do anything with you He pleases? Are you wholly available to Him?

One day the Brown family were really thrilled, for their first car arrived at the front door. Excitedly, the children rushed out to look it over and take turns at sitting behind the steering

112

wheel pretending to drive. 'Really, Dad, it's great. How on earth did you manage to afford it?' Dad just smiled quietly.

What he wasn't telling the children was that he hadn't bought it at all. In reality he couldn't afford a car and this one actually belonged to the children's aunt. She was a generous soul and she paid for the car, garaged it and said to Mr Brown: 'It's yours to use. Enjoy it. Take the children to the seaside, or into the country. The only condition is that I will have the car when I really need it.'

Mostly, that was fine. The Brown family felt glad to have the car at all. There were just some times though when Mr Brown had a plan to do something but had to back down because aunty needed it. After all, she owned the car and so she had to have it if she wanted.

Similarly some people think they can be like 'aunty' in their arrangement with Jesus. 'Yes, Jesus, here is my life. You can have it — it's yours. Do with me as you please... Except, that is, you must understand that there'll be times when I'll want my life back again. If ever I think I know best... If ever you demand something from me I don't want to give... At moments like that you'll have to realise you must release me. After all, I still own my life.'

Jesus' understanding of discipleship is rather different — see Luke 14:33.

Suffering . . .

Bethan Lloyd-Jones, widow of Martyn, tells of a trip they took in Canada in the summer of 1932. At one stage they travelled by train through beautiful, hilly, wooded country. They journeyed along one side of a valley and Bethan's eyes marvelled at the dark green conifers covering the opposite hillside.

Then she noticed that right in the middle of the front row of trees was one different from the rest. It glowed with a gold, red colour and looked very attractive against the dark background.

She asked a friend the name of such a tree and remarked on its beauty. 'Yes,' he said, 'It does look good there but it is quite dead, you know. It will stay like that for the summer but it will be broken to bits by the ice and snow and gales when the hard weather comes — there's no life in it.' (Bethan Lloyd-Jones, Memories of Sandfields, Banner of Truth Trust, Edinburgh, 1983, p.54.)

And so, we can all look marvellous on the outside when things are going well — when the 'sunshine' is out in our lives. It's easy to be a wonderful Christian then. The real test comes though in the 'winter-time' of suffering or hardship — that's what reveals whether or not we have the real life of Jesus to sustain and keep us.

If you buy an electric shower, you would be wise to buy one with a protection against overheating. For an electric shower doesn't heat the water in a tank but heats cold water as it passes through a narrow pipe just before it goes to the shower head. Under normal circumstances that's fine and there's no problem. As long as the flow of water is constant, you can adjust the controls to give the right heat for a comfortable shower.

If, however, if someone elsewhere in the house turns on a cold tap, the water pressure reaching the shower unit will suddenly decrease. If, then, there is less water passing through the same heating unit, it may at that moment be heated almost to scalding point — and standing under the shower suddenly becomes much less pleasant, and possibly dangerous.

Therefore the better showers are fitted with a safety overheat protection. In other words, if the water reaches too high a temperature, the heating element is automatically reduced or switched off and so it is impossible to be burned. When the temperature is too hot, the system automatically cools it down.

Many Christians think naively that that should happen automatically for Christians faced with difficulty or danger. They imagine there's some automatic pressure release from trouble — a kind of evangelical shut-off valve which means they'll never find their nerves on edge or their blood-pressure raised. Yet the Scriptures have no promise of any automatic release from pressure.

The wise parent knows that he cannot always solve his child's problems for him. Sometimes, with the parent's support and encouragement, the child must simply battle through. He must face the challenge, accept the knocks and learn the lessons. He will never grow up properly in a tough world if he doesn't learn how to do that.

God too does not automatically lift us out of every difficulty, because He wants His children to grow up. His strength and grace to cope are always there but He doesn't simply snap His fingers and take away all our problems.

Most married men will have had a few experiences of being left alone. One man's wife may have needed a trip to see her family at a special occasion. Another's wife may have gone to a conference. Many will have been left while the wife became a mother, lying for a few days in the maternity hospital.

All honest men will admit these are sobering times! These are the days when you realise that no matter how competent you thought yourself to be, you find that as a mere mortal — and particularly as a mere mortal man — you cannot manage alone.

The point is that the husband's awareness of the need of his wife may only become that clear when her companionship and assistance are removed for a time.

There are times when God, while never abandoning us, lets us feel our need of Him. We suffer and feel we're about to go under but then God scoops us up with His hand as we realise again how lost we would be without Him. (2 Corinthians 1:8-9).

116

Suffering can be a means of moulding character.

A minister was called to visit an old woman, lying alone in an attic bedroom. He was told that this woman had been crippled for years, her body racked with pain through arthritis and other disabilities. Life had been very hard and cruel for her.

In the light of this information, he decided to take her a small gift of a booklet which was full of hope. It was a simple booklet which encouraged people to place their faith in God no matter their circumstances, to have patience and to trust Him. It was a tremendous testimony to God's goodness and mercy.

The minister visited the old woman and gave the book to her, saying: 'I believe this booklet might be relevant to your situation.'

'Yes it is,' she said, 'I wrote it.'

Some changes in our characters can emerge only from the crucible of suffering.

Romans 5:3, 'We rejoice in our sufferings, because we know that suffering produces perseverance...'

Suffering can be God's means of moulding and shaping your life to make you more like His Son. It shows that you matter to Him, and the very thing which is a trial to you, a burden to you, is God's good means of transforming your life.

If a diamond had feelings, it would go through agony as it is ground, shaped and polished. It would be painful to have all those rough edges knocked off and then to have high-speed abrasive pads remove excess layers of dirt and imperfection.

Yet it is because the jeweller values the diamond that he treats it in that way. Only by such means can it become the true thing of beauty which is its potential.

Likewise God does not allow suffering to discourage or harm you but because He cares for you enough to bring you to the full stature of the child of God that you were always meant to have.

See 1 Peter 4:14 and Matthew 5:11-12.

Suffering should lead you to trust yourself to God.

When a patient allows himself to be operated on, superficially he is doing something very foolish. He's allowing someone to take a knife and stab him... So why does he permit that?

The patient allows it because he trusts that

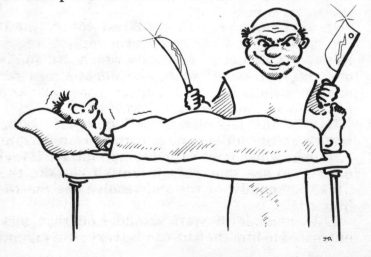

every such act by the surgeon is actually for his good. Yes, of course the surgeon must cut the flesh, and that — in a sense — is to inflict suffering on the body. He does it though only in order to bring about an even higher good eventually, perhaps the removal of a troublesome appendix, or a tumour.

The patient believes the surgeon knows what he is doing and therefore entrusts himself into his hands.

See 1 Peter 4:19.

The simple message here is that, when suffering comes, don't give up. Rather, all the more firmly entrust yourself into the strong arms of God. He loves you and He knows what He is doing.

A joyful acceptance of suffering is possible.

In a business, delegation is one of the hardest things for a boss to do.

If an employer is determined to try, he'll probably begin with delegating routine tasks. Next he'll delegate decisions which are fairly obvious — then delegate the negotiations for easy contracts — then harder contracts and harder decisions. So on it'll go.

One of the last things he'll delegate is the responsibility of dealing with an important customer who comes with a complaint. He'll feel obliged to see that person himself — take the 'flak' personally — try and resolve the matter himself.

If a member of staff should find that task entrusted to him then he can be very sure indeed that his boss has a lot of confidence in him.

What can God allow into our lives? Can He entrust us even with suffering and know that we will not curse but still praise Him?

See 1 Peter 4:13 and Acts 5:41.

In the latter passage the apostles realise that God is not only willing to allow them to witness and share the good news of Jesus but God is willing to allow them to be accused on His behalf. He's willing to allow them to take the brunt of the world's opposition to the gospel.

The disciples saw that as a great privilege. They hadn't 'arrived' but they were clearly becoming better and better servants for God. He could entrust yet more to them. All the more they were being identified with God's Son.

Temptation . . .

Temptation, of course, can be resisted. But, if that is to be done, two things are required:
— that we are walking full of the Holy Spirit and therefore close to God;
— that we fill our minds with God's Word.

Both of these lead to an awareness of what is from God and what is simply a product of our own evil desires, spurred on by Satan.

If many of us had been in Jesus' shoes when He was tempted, faced with such convincing arguments by Satan, we'd have believed him and gone along with his plans.

Jesus, however, was walking with God and He knew the Scriptures completely. So, although Satan was able to lift verses out of their context for his argument, Jesus knew what God really wanted and could answer Satan back from the Scriptures.

For an army to win a battle, it must have the confidence that its weapons are stronger than the enemy's, and, of course, it must know how to fire them. Then it'll see the victory.

But if it doubts its own resources then it'll probably not even fight because it'll be so convinced of losing. It'll simply surrender.

God has not left His people defenceless. He has given His Holy Spirit and given us His Word.

We cannot use them though if we do not know them.

If you are to learn to do something then that's only possible from someone who knows about that subject.

So, I wouldn't go to a single person for lessons on how to be happily married and he wouldn't come to me for instruction on how to play par golf!

We learn only from those who have first mastered the relevant subject.

That is why we can turn to Jesus when we face temptation — that universal problem which none of us can escape. Jesus knows what it is like to be tempted — He's experienced it — and He's won through it. See Hebrews 4:15-16.

Jesus knows and so He can help us.

Testing . . .

When a couple take their wedding vows, they promise to keep those vows and to be committed to each other until death parts them. Their relationship is permanent.

Now those vows are fine, but the proof of their genuineness is whether the marriage will last through times of difficulty — illness, poverty, temptation to another person, etc. The evidence that the initial commitment is real is that it is still valid after a time of trial.

One reason why trials and difficulties come into our lives is so that our faith may be proved genuine, that it may be shown to last. See 1 Peter 1:6-7.

Suffering because of faith sorts out priorities and forces us to choose God's ways.

Suppose a young man is lined up by his father to succeed him in the family business. That's always been the father's ambition for his son. It's important, he feels, to keep the firm within the family, and the son has never disagreed with that aim.

Now, however, the son feels led by God to train for the ministry. He has a sense of call, and can do no other than to prepare himself for full-time Christian service. Inevitably, that will make it impossible for him to take over the firm when his father retires.

That news is devastating to the father. He does

not share the son's faith and pleads and persuades as much as he can to get the young man to change his mind. The son though remains resolute. Finally, the father says: 'If that's your choice, then you're not acting like any son of mine. So you're no longer welcome in this house and I shall see my lawyer to make sure the inheritance goes elsewhere.'

The son is hurt badly, not at the thought of the financial loss but at the loss of relationship with the father he loves. Yet, for him the call of God is not negotiable and, no matter the price, he must still follow that leading into the ministry.

Now, see the point: Through the suffering of making that choice, the son is able once and for all to overcome a potential sin — that of putting an earthly father's wishes before those of the heavenly Father. Jesus said no-one was to have a higher claim on a disciple than God. That issue freed him from that sin.

This kind of suffering, or testing, sorts out our lives in a way nothing else can. Because of it, we either sink in sin or rise high to triumph over sin. See 1 Peter 4:1.

Trust . . .

A wife knows that her husband truly trusts her driving when, on a long car journey, he lets her take the wheel while he drops off to sleep. The ability to relax reveals trust.

If we can't relax about the situations we face in life, what does that say about our trust — or lack of it — in God?

Trust means letting go and allowing Jesus to deal with something, not constantly interfering yourself.

If you buy some electrical gadget, you'll get a guarantee with it. If you read that, it'll tell you what to do if something goes wrong — how to wrap it up, where to send it, etc.

Almost certainly it will also tell you that the guarantee is null and void if you try and repair the gadget yourself. The firm will not accept responsibility for the product if you interfere with it. Either they are dealing with the problem, or you are — both can't.

The same principle applies with the faults and problems in your life. Either Jesus is being allowed to deal with them, or you're taking responsibility yourself.

Trust means believing Jesus can handle a matter better than we are able to, and that is often the problem.

Some businesses virtually go 'bust' because of a managing director who refuses to accept anyone else's judgment over against his own. He knows best:
— how the product should be advertised;
— how many staff are needed for each job;
— how much money should be allocated to future research;
— whether a particular product has exhausted its usefulness or not;
— Etc.

He'd never dream of employing an advertising agency, or accepting the opinion of his qualified staff.

He does not trust even those more expert than himself.

Surely we are not to be like that as Christians? Jesus, our expert, should be our first resort.

Truth . . .

A boy had an essay to write for school but he decided to get some help. He went to his mother, and asked: 'Mum, how was I born?' 'Oh,' she replied, 'the stork just flew past and dropped you down our chimney'.

He moved on to his grandmother. 'Granny, how was my mummy born?' Granny also said: 'The stork just flew past and dropped her down the chimney.'

Then he asked: 'And, Granny, how were you born?' 'The stork just flew past and dropped me down the chimney.'

So the boy began his essay: 'There has not been a natural birth in our family for three generations...'

Sometimes we don't help others by our unwillingness to tell the truth...

Unity . . .

A very serious medical condition occurs when the body has an internal 'war', as the body's defence systems get the 'wrong' message and begin to destroy cells in the blood, or some transplanted organ. At the very least, a person in this condition is seriously ill and may well die.

Likewise 'war' in the body of Christ is no less serious. Members fighting with each other weaken a church and can lead to its death.

Urgency . . .

The danger is to say: 'Well, this gospel sounds very fine. But not yet. Not right now. There are too many other things which interest me at present. Maybe one day — when I feel the need of salvation — then I'll come to Jesus.'

And that attitude can be fatal.

Sammy Squirrel had a good summer. Every day he played with his little squirrel friends. They ran, they jumped, they hid from the curious human beings who sometimes pointed in their direction. If they came too near, Sammy would scurry up a tree and hide among the branches, or dive into a hole in the trunk. It was a great life as a squirrel.

Just occasionally some words of wisdom he'd

heard came back to him, that he really ought to gather some nuts for winter.

But the sun was still shining and Sammy told himself: 'Winter's still a long way off. I'd rather play some more.' So off he would go to amuse himself for another day. With practice it wasn't all that difficult to suppress the inner urge to prepare for winter.

However, one day Sammy woke up and shivered. He was cold. Out of his hole he popped and — to his amazement — the ground was covered in snow. 'This must be winter,' he told himself. 'I'd better gather some nuts together.'

But Sammy soon learned the terrible truth that you can't find nuts under six inches of snow. No matter how hard he tried, he couldn't find even one. Sammy hadn't thought it important to do anything to be ready for winter. He had no food. So Sammy died.

There are people who think it of no great importance that they keep suppressing the inner urge to obey God, to accept His will for their lives, to follow His call now.

Think how tragic it would be to waken up one day to find 'winter' had come and you weren't ready. It'll be too late then to start thinking about God and deciding about His Son, Jesus.

This is the only moment we have to get prepared. There are no guarantees beyond right now. 'Winter' is coming... Get ready!

Vision . . .

You could take someone to the most beautiful spot in the world but if he is blind then the beauty will mostly be lost on him.

There are also people, even within the church, who are spiritually blind. They cannot see that God wants anything of them as Christians. They cannot see the need for personal change, nor for their part in the work of the Body of Christ.

Go to the centre of a large city and look around. How far can you see? The answer will be 'Not very far'. Why is that? Is there something wrong with your eyes?

No, the eyesight is fine. It's just that there are too many large buildings — stores, office blocks — which are in the way and spoil the view.

Now go to the seashore and look around there. Suddenly you can see for miles, right out to a distant horizon. And this time it's because there are no obstructions.

Many Christians have no vision of God's purposes for their lives, or for this world, because they have allowed their lives to become over-crowded with things which are not from God. They fill their lives and minds with relationships, literature, TV programmes, or other activities which 'spoil the view'. There just isn't enough 'space' left in their lives for God's vision to be seen by them.

When I was about fourteen I went to a Boy Scout camp on the shores of Loch Tummel, near

Pitlochry, Scotland. One day we walked to Queen's View, named after Queen Victoria who loved to stand there and admire one of the most glorious views in all the Scottish Highlands.

To me that scene, with the loch stretched out below, islands dotted here and there and the dark hills beyond, was quite magnificent. Something stirred within me at the sight.

That would be true for about half of the boys who were with me. We stood, staring and staring. The other half, however, looked for all of five seconds and then wandered off to find something more useful and interesting to do.

Now, in one sense, they saw what the rest of us saw but in another sense they didn't see it at all. They had never been brought up to appreciate the beauty of the countryside. Perhaps the latest and most sophisticated piece of technology would have got their attention. Certainly the scenic panorama was lost on them.

Likewise people who are not trained by the example of others, and in God's Word and in prayer, miss the largest and grandest of visions God puts before them.

That may rob them of real worship, for Christ's death for their sins means little more to them than an efficient means to their salvation and they cannot understand how some can be 'lost in wonder, love and praise'. Or they may miss God's vision of His church reaching out into the world. To them the world is simply a place to be shunned and they cannot 'see' the Father's heart of love and hand of grace reaching out through His people to win the lost to Himself.

Such Christians read the same words and hear the same sermons but they lack the vision.

Warning . . .

A philosopher has illustrated the situation of our world this way.

Imagine there has been a mini ice-age, a time of great coldness on the face of the earth. During that time, a nomadic tribe has pitched its camp on the frozen surface of a lake. The ice is many feet thick and can easily bear their weight.

Each day now the sun shines and every night the tribesmen light huge braziers on the ice to provide heat. Gradually that ice is melting and becoming thinner.

Yet the tribesmen can't see any difference and with no awareness of danger they carry on living where they are. One day soon the ice will give way. The only question is 'when?'.

God warns us of that kind of complacency as our world moves steadily nearer to its end. Unaware of any danger, simply taking what pleasure can be found from each day, men and women blithely ignore the danger they are in as strangers to God.

It was like that just before the flood destroyed all but Noah and his family, and Jesus said the same naive living, as if there was nothing about which to be concerned, would characterise the days before his return (Matthew 24:36-39). Be warned! Make peace with God while there is still time.

A man comes home and finds his pet dog has chewed his slippers to pieces earlier that day. He

133

calls out to the dog: 'Fido, come here.' Obediently Fido trots over to his master, tail wagging. Wallop! The dog is belted across the nose.

Now, is that man's slippers likely to be any safer the next day? Answer: Not at all, for the dog had no way of knowing it was being punished for that act. Indeed, the man is more likely to find

that Fido is reluctant to come when called as he'll probably associate that with the wallop he received.

To be effective, a punishment must be understood.

That's one reason why, before God ever sent any punishment on Israel, He gave them messengers, prophets, to explain their sin to them and warn them of potential consequences.

Worship . . .

We often confuse true worship with the forms of worship.

It's Fred Bloggs' wedding anniversary. Fred's remembered alright, but he has a problem. As a family, they're absolutely broke at this time. There really is no money available except for essentials.

Fred though truly loves the missus, so out he goes at six in the morning to the garden and he picks a small bunch of flowers. He puts them in a vase and makes her breakfast. Then he puts her tea and toast on a tray, the vase of flowers beside it and up he goes with it all to the bedroom to waken her. Just after he's left for work later, Mrs Bloggs finds a little note from Fred telling her how much he loves her. Believe me, she knows that, after all these years of marriage, his love for her is still there.

It's Joe Soap's anniversary as well. He's remembered too, but only because his wife wrote it in his diary at the beginning of the year. He doesn't have time to say much to his wife in the morning because he's rushing off to work. Joe works almost constantly all the time and so there's been very little time with his wife over the years. At one point, however, during that day, the doorbell at home goes and Mrs Soap finds it's the man from Interflora with the most enormous bunch of very expensive flowers. Her heart leaps for a moment, but when she reads the note, she finds her husband's secretary has written it on his behalf. Later in the day she 'phones her husband to remind him about their special meal out but he says he's going to have to work late again and so the meal is cancelled. Joe knows he's behaved rather badly, so when he comes in about eleven that night, he brings an expensive new coat for his wife as an anniversary present. All he can do, however, is leave it for her, since she's already gone to bed.

Mrs Soap got a large and expensive floral bouquet delivered to her door and a brand new coat as a present.

Mrs Bloggs got a bunch of flowers from the garden and a note from her husband.

In terms of the trappings of an anniversary, Mrs Soap did rather well compared to Mrs Bloggs but I wonder which one of them felt really loved...?

The answer to that is clear.

Well, let it be just as clear when it comes to worship.

God is concerned about our attitudes in worship. We've become preoccupied about the expressions or forms of worship.

The truth is that any expression of worship is empty if there is no inner attitude to match. If all we have is a form of worship, perhaps out of habit, then there's no offering to God and therefore nothing acceptable to Him.

Do you know what most of you are really good at doing? I mean something at which you're positively accomplished?

You're almost all really good at cleaning your teeth. It doesn't matter if you take your teeth out to do it, or you're able to keep them in your mouth, most of you will give them a scrub at least once a day. Now you've probably been doing that since you first had teeth, which means you've cleaned them thousands and thousands of times.

So it wasn't difficult for you to clean your teeth this morning, (if you did), or to do it tonight, because it's normal and natural behaviour for you.

Lots of people wonder why they can't enter into a real time of praise in church. And the answer is that they could if only they would give God at least as much attention as they do their teeth!

People ignore worshipping God, focusing on His beauty and splendour, declaring His greatness and worth, from one week to the next, and then are surprised that they can't just turn on, tune in and sense His presence on a Sunday.

Do you know, there was a time when I couldn't find one good thing to say about my wife? There was nothing there at all.

You might find that shocking, but I would have to be honest and say that situation went on for quite a number of years... No feeling, no emotion...

In fact it went on for precisely twenty one years... And then I met her. You see, I couldn't say anything good about someone I didn't know!

If you were to ask me now what she is like, I could extol her virtues for a long time. Now I know her. I spend time every day with her and every day appreciate something new about her.

If you asked me to praise someone else, I'd struggle because I'm not in anyone else's company for very long at all and I simply wouldn't know very much to say.

You can extol only someone you know and with whom you spend time.

So, you can't expect to arrive in church and be swept away in a wonderful expression of praise to God if you don't really know Him as the loving Father He is, and if you haven't taken time to worship Him already this week.

For so many, the principal focus of a church service is always on what man can get from God. Never is it on what man can give to God.

Can you imagine how God feels about that?

Suppose a woman told her husband that the only reason she lived with him was because of his good income which provided her with lots of things she wanted.

How would he feel about that?

Now if we only come before God to 'get', then we're almost saying something as bad as that to Him.
